SHATTERED DREAMS

AND

BROKEN HEARTS

FENTANYL, THE KILLER

A FAMILY'S WORST NIGHTMARE

Sylvia Abolis Mennear

Given the powerful story and relevant information included by Sylvia in Shattered Dreams and Broken Hearts, I rate it 4 out of 4 stars. The author includes useful detail about illicit drugs and their effects, a copy of the coroner's report for Aaron, and notes from both Aaron and his girlfriend Shauna about his experiences. Her research makes it clear that the problem of illicit drug death in British Columbia is worsening at an alarming rate. I would recommend this book to all parents of children around their teens or anyone else affected by a drug problem. Just be warned: it is a heart-wrenching emotional journey. We all like to think this couldn't happen to us, but Sylvia and her family are living proof it could happen to anyone.

joshfee77 - onlinebookclub.org

What I have liked about this book is that it's based on a true story....I also admire that the mother shared about her son's situation which is very rare some of them like to keep it a secret afraid of what people will say.

lavisha - onlinebookclub.org

Excellent. I found this book is more advanced in educating the young people of today who abuse drugs through Aaron's life incidents. It was unfortunate that he could not conduct the life savers program. But however the death of Aaron may change lots of lives. I give 4/4 for this book.

Stalin Muthuswamy - onlinebookclub.org

I can imagine how much emotion was poured into the compilation of this book The author has done well in getting this work out for many to read, it would be one to save numerous lives. Thank you..

Dahmy10 - onlinebookclub.org

I am so glad to hear about this book. I think stories like this are what is needed for addiction to be more fully understood. It can literally happen to anyone. I will look for this book! Your review is very well written and comprehensive. Thanks!

Eva Darrington - onlinebookclub.org

SHATTERED DREAMS

AND

BROKEN HEARTS

<u>Also by Sylvia Abolis Mennear</u>

Enchanted Castle on the River
'Matt's Journey'

I am dedicating this book to my son Aaron James
7/7/86 - 4/19/17
and
my niece Emily Beverley
9/24/83 - 5/24/17

and all the other victims of opiates and this horrible drug called
Fentanyl.
It is no longer a drug strictly used by drug addicts, but
unsuspecting people who would never even think of taking
something so harmful.

We have to put an end to this crisis! We are losing a whole
generation of people and it's tearing apart our families.

I decided to write this book because if I can turn just one person
away from taking these killing drugs, then I have done the work
my son was trying to start. Through a spiritual medium my son
told me to write, and this was after my husband and sister told
me to start a diary. I didn't think I could go through with it, but
I gave it a lot of consideration and realized that I should—and I
have to do it—for Aaron's sake. It's the last thing I can do for
my son.

I love my son Aaron more than I can express. He has been gone
now for almost four months when I started this book. Not a day
goes by that I don't think about Aaron and shed tears. My heart
aches for his physical being and I have so much hate for the

people distributing this poison. We have to find a global way to put a stop to it!

Some of the proceeds from each book sold will be donated to MSTH; momsstoptheharm.com.

I am also writing this book with hopes that it will be a sort of healing therapy for myself.

AARON

A - April 19th your soul departed,
you left your family broken hearted

A - Answers we will never get,
why the angels thought best you left

R - Reality won't set in that you're physically gone,
my motherly instinct keeps grabbing on

O - Our time together was much too short,
my life without you I cannot support

N - Not a day goes by you're not on my mind,
I love you so much, son of mine!

Sylvia Abolis Mennear, 2017

<u>DAY ONE</u>

Day One

April 19, 2017: Brother Daniel's 28th Birthday

It was 10:00 a.m. on that Wednesday. I was sweeping the floor, trying to clean up the house, as we were expecting a realtor to come and view the house that we had put up for sale.

I said to my youngest son, Daniel, "I can't believe Aaron is still sleeping. I had better go wake him up; the realtor will be here within an hour."

I leaned the broom against the kitchen bar and walked to his bedroom door. I knocked on the door and called his name: "Aaron . . . Aaron . . ." No answer. He must be in a deep sleep. I opened his door; the room was dark. I called his name again, "Aaron . . ." My heart skipped a beat. Something was not right as I walked up to him.

I looked at his face and I knew right away he was gone, deceased. I thought I would myself perish on the spot. I screamed as loud as I had ever screamed in my life. When I was out of breath, I screamed again. I heard my youngest son, Daniel, in the kitchen, yell out: "What?" and then I heard the kitchen chair slide and he came running into Aaron's room. Next I heard Jim, my husband, yelling something, and he came running into Aaron's room.

Daniel's first words were, "Oh my God, Aaron! No!"

When Jim came running in, he also yelled, "Oh my God!" I can't remember verbatim, because my thoughts were engulfed in looking at my dead son, not what the others were saying. Jim said, "Check his pulse."

I yelled, "I did, and he is stone cold! He has been gone for hours! Call 9-1-1!"

We had never been through anything like this before, and were in such shock that we really did not know what to do first. As Jim left Aaron's room in a state of confusion and grief, I sat on Aaron's bed and cried and kissed him and just held him. Then I looked up at the ceiling and yelled at God. "How could you take him from us? He is so young, and has his whole life ahead of him!" I'm a Catholic, and I had never in my life been so angry with God as I was that day. Our children are not supposed to leave this world before us!

I lost my faith in that instant. How could there be a God if he didn't give me a sign that there was something wrong? How could there be a God if he could let my son die like this?

We did not know at the time how he had died, but we knew he had aspirated during the night because there was vomit all down his face and on his chest. *So why didn't God roll him to his side? Why didn't God make him wake up when he was vomiting?* He had clearly choked on it. His cell phone was sitting facedown on his chest. His left eye and mouth were partially open. His face looked so thin; his nostrils were almost completely squeezed together—and he had a shirt tie wrapped around his forehead, which took us by surprise.

While Jim was in the kitchen making phone calls and yelling back asking questions, I got mad because 9-1-1 was asking Jim if Aaron had a pulse and so on. I yelled, "I already said no! He is partially blue, stiff, and stone-cold; he has been gone for hours. Just tell them to get out here!" I couldn't believe I was describing my son. This was a nightmare, and I desperately wanted to wake up. I would have traded my life for Aaron's, no question. I even told God to please take me instead; *"I have lived a good life, Aaron has only lived half a life. He is a good boy and doesn't deserve this!"*

My life was over! I know Daniel and Jim felt the same way. Jim had also called and asked our dear friends Al and Darlene to come out. Darlene and Al had lost a son several years before, at the age of 19. Darlene and Al also volunteer for the organization The Compassionate Friends, so they would understand and be able to help us, because they had already gone through something similar with their son. Also, Aaron was like a son to them, and they loved him. Al and Darlene are like family to us, and since the rest of our family live a 5- or 8-hour drive away, we had no one else we would feel comfortable being with.

When Jim called 9-1-1, and because he told them that Aaron had passed away with no knowledge of why or how, they sent out two police vehicles, an ambulance, and a family services representative, plus the coroner. The paramedics wore hazmat suits because they did not know what they were dealing with; it could have been a case of airborne particles. It did upset me to the core; my son was being treated like he was toxic. When they arrived, they didn't want any of us near Aaron because if there were drugs involved, like Fentanyl, then it could be airborne, and very hazardous for anyone in the room. I told them I didn't care; he is my son, and my life is over anyway. I was furious with them. *How dare they tell me I can't stay with my son, my flesh, my blood, my heart!* I stayed with him until they asked me to leave so they could clean him up, and then we could come back in.

———————

AARON'S STORY

(Aaron's own words... found in a folder after he passed away, has not been edited)

On the morning of Saturday January 11, 2014, I set out to Jasper Marmot Basin, Alberta for a snowboard trip that unknowingly would end in complete disaster. The snow was falling hard, as there was a storm slowly sweeping in during my drive to the mountains. As I arrived at the hill the day was growing brighter and there was not a single set of tracks on the ski hill yet. I spend a good 6 hours riding in waist high powder, making up for the last 6 years of no snowboarding. Nearing the end of the day, I decided to do 1 more run ending in the freestyle snowboard park. As I prepared myself for the final jump of the day, I noticed I was quite fatigued from the day of boarding, but that quickly changed when a favourite song of mine came on through my headphones. I crouched down and gained speed towards the jump. As I let off the tip of the kicker, I then realized my perception was way out and I had hit the jump with too much speed. Flailing through the air from 15 feet up I knew the landing was going to be horrible. I lost my balance and was leaning forwards as I came closer to the ground. On impact, my left leg touched down first and I heard a loud crack through the deepest parts of my ear canal. I tried to stand up but fell back down and was in incredible pain. I then assessed my situation and patted down my leg, which then I realized I had a bone sticking out of my leg.

In and out of consciousness due to shock and pain, it took nearly 45 min for someone to finally stop and get help. I was rush to the Jasper hospital where my first of 4 surgeries was performed. They tried to put my tibia back in place for the travel back to Edmonton, but was having very little luck. I was placed into an ambulance and then escorted to the Misiricorida hospital in West Edmonton, where I was then to undergo my second surgery of the day.

The following morning, I woke up in a complete confusion and anxiety realizing that everything that had happened was not a nightmare. I looked down at my leg and noticed many metal rods sticking out of my leg. They had installed an external fixator, on my tibia to keep it in place until the swelling went down to which they could then perform my 3rd surgery. A week went by where I experienced some real low times in my life with depression, extreme pain and a feeling of failure. The pain killers were not helping my mental state, as I seemed to fade and forget about all my problems surrounding me. I had spent the 4 years prior to my injury building myself and my body so I could one day stand on stage amongst all my other competitors (body builders). I understood that this injury was going to be a long and difficult process, and maybe one of the most difficult mental hurdles I would ever have to overcome. A week later I was put in for another surgery, where I had the fixator removed and three titanium plates mounted along my tibia to hold it together. I had found that I had broke my tibia in six places, dislocated my knee, injured my acl, mcl, IT band, and my meniscus.

After months of physio therapy and being wheelchair bound, by the end of March I was finally able to try and take my first steps again assisted with a cane. I had no idea it would be so difficult to try and walk, as I had lost all the mobility in my left leg and dropped over fifty pounds in sixteen days of being in the hospital. My road to recovery was an extremely painful experience, both mental and physical, but I had set myself a goal, that when I was able to walk properly and had healed enough, that I would finally work towards stepping on stage and competing in the ABBA Northern Body Building Contest.

By the middle of July I was able to return to work on modified duties, as well return to the gym and begin my journey to the stage. Months went by where I went through a lot of physical changes and pain in my left leg, as I tried to gain the range of motion back in my left leg. By October I figured my leg was healed enough that I shouldn't be experiencing anymore pain, but unfortunately my leg was still causing a lot of discomfort. After multiple doctors appointments, we had found that one of the pins that went horizontal through the largest party of my knee, was protruding through the bone and pushing out my skin. December fifth I was to finally undergo (hopefully) my final surgery, in which they removed one plate from my leg and the pin that was causing the pain.

The plate stretched over twelve inches long, was shaped to fit my knee and had nearly two dozen holes in it where it could be attached to my bone.

On January first 2015, I began my diet and training so that I could compete on May seventeenth in the ABBA Northern Bodybuilding Contest. I went through many hard times in my journey, but looked back at my times in a wheelchair and used that to motivate me through the hardships of my diet and training. I pushed more harder than I ever had in my life, and dedicated every breathing second of my day to make sure I would be stepping on stage in five months. I had amazing support from family and friends to help guide me through the harder times of my contest preparation.

The Alberta Body Building Association was so impressed with Aaron that they did an article on him.

Alberta Body Building Association

https://www.facebook.com/Albertabodybuildingassociation/photos/a.791
868707575594.1073741848.346092832153186/796338227128642/?type
=3&theaterMay 19, 2015 ·

An incredible story of triumph hit the Northerns Stage this weekend.
A before and after shot from January 2014 to May 2015. He was
unable to walk for 7 months after a snowboarding accident. Aaron
Mennear shared his story with me and it serves us all well to be
reminded how blessed we all really are to even be able to pursue our
dreams and get on stage. Thank you for sharing Aaron - clearly there
is more than a trophy to be won.

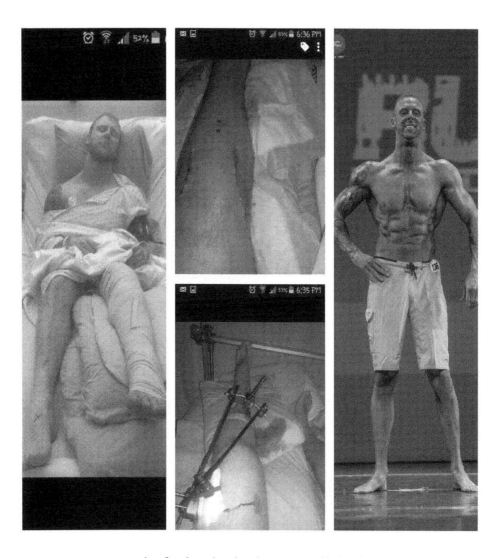

We were so proud of what he had accomplished. We were not excited that he was going into bodybuilding, because of what he had to endure, but we were so proud of him.

After a couple of Aaron's surgeries, and before his bodybuilding, he flew home to heal. He was in a bad state Jim said that during the drive home from the airport, just over an hour, Aaron barely talked; he was in a depression. It killed me to see him this way, but I was so glad he was home. Home to get healed.

We rented him a wheelchair and several other medical hardware items that he needed. He stayed with us for several months. It was so difficult seeing him like this, because he was never a person that could just sit still. He was always on the move, doing something. Now he was wheelchair-bound and in so much pain. He was getting upset that we had to do everything for him; he never wanted people to dote on him. He loved helping other people, but he liked doing his own things for himself. It was a very harsh several months, with depression setting in.

We had already booked a trip to Mexico for a few months and decided that we would still go because our younger son was at home and would help take care of him. I also had our neighbour girl, Kayla, a wonderful person, come and check on him every day. She also took him to physio and the doctor and anywhere else he had to go. He truly appreciated her, yet he was also feeling so low. Saying he didn't need a babysitter. We were so grateful for her.

After a few months, he felt good enough to go back home. I really didn't want him to go, but he wanted so desperately to go back to work and start on his bodybuilding regimen. So he left. He brought home a Ziploc bag full of meds for pain, and I also found out that someone back in Alberta was mailing him injectable steroids, and who knows what else. I would ask him, "Aaron, how can you take so many pills? These could kill you."

He's say, "Don't worry, Mom, they are all prescribed from the doctor in Alberta, and I only take the pain meds when I need them." Right . . . several times, he told me the pills weren't working so he would take more than the allotted amount at one time.

No matter what I said about the usage of the meds, it was like talking to a stone wall.

There were some details of this journey of Aaron's that he did not include in his writings. Details that we found out through his friends, his ex-girlfriend, and his current girlfriend. I would like to share some of this with you, so you can understand what led him to the destruction of himself. But before I do that, I would like to tell you about Aaron as a healthy person, without the drugs.

Aaron James was born July 7, 1986, in New Westminster, British Columbia. He was a beautiful, happy baby; he was such a joy, hardly gave us any problems. Always smiling or laughing. His smile lit up a room. Growing up, he always had a lot of friends and made friends so easily. He was always there to help people. If someone got hurt, he would be there right away to help. Everything he attempted to do, he did well. He loved baseball, and played for 13 years. He was a great pitcher and batter, and excelled in skateboarding, snowboarding, wakeboarding, fishing, hiking, karate, piano, drums, drawing, and so much more. He loved to do anything outdoors.

I remember his first day of kindergarten. When he came home, his teacher called me and asked me to have a talk with Aaron because he tried to kiss a girl under the table. I laughed so hard because it was so funny, and even up to his adult age, he was always a ladies' man. He loved women, especially his current girlfriend, Shauna; he always wanted to impress her. He was my little man, always full of emotion. Sometimes I thought he should have been born a girl, because he would get very emotional and sensitive.

He hated spiders. One day in Edmonton he was in his basement suite, studying for an exam, and he saw a spider on the wall above his head. He actually called the landlady upstairs to come down and get rid of it. We asked him, "Weren't you embarrassed asking her?"

He said, "No, I couldn't kill it; it's too gross, and I wanted it out of here. They freak me out."

As a child and through his growing years, he was always so sensitive to other people. If he accidentally hurt his younger brother, he would be devastated. I remember a time when they were play fighting and Daniel got hurt and started to cry. Aaron quickly hugged him and said, "I'm so sorry, Daniel! Where does it hurt?" He would always own up to the fact that it was he that hurt Daniel. He wouldn't lie and say that he fell or he didn't know how it happened. I know Aaron would have been an excellent and devoted parent if he'd had the chance.

Sometimes I think this world was just too cruel for Aaron's soul.

He loved making presents for us at school, from kindergarten through to high school. Everything he made was made with so much love. Aaron was on the honour roll several times from elementary school through high school—until his life changed somewhere between grades 8 and 9. I understand now why so many parents do homeschooling. It helps to keep their kids pure, and out of harm's way from the kids that love to socialize in a bad way (i.e., drugs, booze). At least until they reach a mature age, and are old enough to understand what the horrific outcome could be. Although there would have to be a happy medium, because a child that is cooped up in his or her house day and night, without any outside stimuli, such as field trips or hanging with friends, could also plunge into the reverse effect quickly because it would look so enjoyable to them. There has to be a balance.

Raising kids is so much harder than we thought when we were young. Our plan was to nurture and love them, watch them learn and achieve, watch them grow, get married, have kids. Basically, have a wonderful life. But somewhere during this journey, my son met some kids that made him believe he wasn't normal or fun to be with if he didn't try some ecstasy. Which would have been in grade 8. At that age, our kids are so vulnerable. He wanted to be with the "in" kids, he wanted to be popular; he didn't want to be a nobody.

I can recall when Aaron was in grade 4 or 5, or maybe grade 6, he got home from school and handed us a blue pill that another child gave him on the bus on the way home. We were so happy that he gave it to us. We took it to the hospital to have it checked out, but unfortunately it got lost, and we have no idea what it was. So it just goes to show it doesn't matter the age of the child, there is always someone out there who is willing to either harm your child or push them into a different way of life. We thought that after our long talk with him about drugs that he would have taken it to heart, and in a serious way. But I guess after a few years of being a teen, the peer pressure got to him.

I found these pages of Aaron's writings on a memory stick in his dresser after he passed away. We were so shocked. My husband and I were great parents. I'm not blowing my horn, it's just the truth. We did everything we thought was right for our kids—kept them so busy in baseball, bowling, swimming, ice skating, snowboarding, karate, piano, boating, camping, holidays, and so much more, so they would not have a chance to get bored and stray. It didn't seem to make a difference, as you will see.

This was all in Aaron's words, I only changed the fonts so it could be read with ease. The date this was written was March 10, 2013, less than a year before his snowboarding accident.

My history

Household

- Grew up in a very loving and stable house hold (1 younger brother, and 1 older half brother, and both parents)

- Was given the things we really desired, and treated amazing

- A very close and active family we were together

- Went on numerous camping, fishing trips, and international vacations

- Was involved in many sports, very athletic

- Growing up, was a bit of a trouble maker, spoke back to the parents, always felt i knew better

- Always tried to over power younger brother, due to older half brother doing the same to me, but when i would hurt him, i felt unbelievably horrible to see the outcome

- From my younger years until present, ive had a hard

- time opening up to my little brother, which i have recently started to speak about my personal issues

- Felt i had to be strong, for the fact that he looked up to me, so i couldnt show weakness or insecurity

- The same issues arose with my family, i would bottle my problems up

Elementary;

- Always felt the need to fit in and get all the attention

- Wasnt bullied, but sometimes the group that was the "cool kids" would single me out. I felt weak, for the most part though we all got along

- Had a good sense of humor which lead to being class clown

- Grades were good

Highschool;

- Began smoking in gr.8, dont know if it was for attention or just enjoyed it

- Smoked marijuana in gr.8 for first time, which i then was introduced to ecstacy

- First use of ecstacy i was hooked by the euphoric feeling and as well the displacement from reality i received

- Would use at parties, school, and home to numb my feelings where i would pour my heart out on paper for hours and hours

- Abused through high school until the age of 19

- Fit in quite well with everyone, but it was still never enough

After graduation;

- My abuse on ecstacy increased drastically

- Would use on normal week days to feel the high, up to

- 13 pills at once

- Was starting to use cocaine

Post secondary;

- Met a girl at my place of work, that was 4 years older and sparked my interest

- Started to see one another, but didnt realize the road ahead

- Cocaine abuse kept us close for the next year and a half

- Dropped out of college 2 weeks before provincials because loss of interest and my addiction

- Was told by my parents they wanted nothing to do with her nor me if i continued my use, as well friends were distancing themselves from me

- At the end of the year and a half i looked at the direction of my life and stopped cold turkey with no rehab or counseling

- I then resorted back to marijuana and heavy drinking

Age 20 until present;

- Met the girl of my dreams (my ex)

- I wanted to do whatever possible to keep her in my life

- Worked harder then anything to get her

- She was stern, and kept me clear of my abuse with cocaine

- Relapsed many times in the last 5 years, mainly due to drinking which would lower my guard

- Many fights after the first 2 years were surfacing due to my issues with failure to express myself, and bottling up my issues

- Felt i had to be a man and deal with them on my own, otherwise i would be judged and embarrassed for bringing forth my problems

- After 2 years, a friend introduced steroids to me

- Prior to this i was fairly confident with myself, but after time started to feel insecure with my figure

- Started to tell myself i needed to get bigger and muscular so my girlfriend at the time would stay with me

- Never considered the fact she became a part of my life

- prior to the use

- With the use i began to tell myself i needed to grow larger and larger so that i could protect her, and make her feel good that she had a muscular and good looking man on her arm

- Started to become more confident in myself and at times feel invincible

- With the use of anabolics my patience wore thin, 90% of our fights were due to my short temper and unreasonable attitude

- Never satisfied with my figure, i abused anabolics and ran them almost straight for 3.5 years up until february 2013

- I left my fiance numerous times for reasons so ridiculous, and caused her so much pain

- I never could understand my actions after they were said and done, due to bottling up my issues, i would then finally explode on her and make rash decisions

- I could only feel hollow and regret, after the pain and grief i put her through, so i once again resorted back to drugs

- I was on a path to destruction and nothing mattered, i didnt care about myself or the decisions i would make, not thinking about the future

- I was with other women during our time apart, and regardless of the things i did, i could only ever compare the other girls to her, and think about her and the mistakes made endlessly

- Time was taken and her huge heart accepted me back on conditions to stop the fighting and try to be more expressive with her

- Things were progressing, until a past promise of the stop usage of anabolics i made, was resurfaced

- Middle of feb.2013 i was coming off a long cycle, and couldnt picture my life without the steroids, so i made an ultimadum and destroyed the best thing i had in my life, i broke off an engagement set in the summer prior, due to the potential loss of my dependant (steroids)

- Some of the issues expressed were my difficulties with feeling comfortable to tell her my problems when they occur, instead of releasing them all at once on her and exploding

- I felt the steroids were always there, and regardless of

- the issues i had in my life, they made things better and me a better person

- Once again alone and filled with pain, regret and anger, i met other women and wouldnt look past the time, to potentially destroying a future with my ex-fiance

- After a weekend of relapsing once again, i was sent a very strong email from my parents telling me that im making a huge mistake, and i better take a look at my life and its path, because im destroying everything and everyone in it

- I was then made aware of my major change in personality over the last few years, from my parents and my brother, notifying me of the differences caused by the steroids

- Pleaded they only wanted their old Aaron back, i hit a hole on my drive home from a weekend of regret and mindless decisions that will haunt me forever

- My ex-fiances mother who has the biggest heart called me, and came to my rescue

- She calmed me down, and made me realize along with the rest of my family that i need to change my life and fix the problems ive made

- The stop of marijuana and steroids have been solid since this day

- After having this sober period without any substances, since the age of 13, urges of past addictions are starting to re-enter my mind and get stronger

- I question all the mistakes ive made towards my ex-fiance and family, and cannot find an answer to my adolescent decisions

- I want to live a happy, healthy, fulfilled life

- I feel like a failure for my path ive chosen, because i would never take advice from my peers, and felt that i could figure lifes complications and influences out on my own

---

I sobbed uncontrollably after reading this. We had no idea. Why didn't he come to us? We told our boys to always come to us when they have a problem. Never feel embarrassed; but he chose not to. I know in the last few months of his life before he came home to live with us, he told his younger brother, Daniel, that he didn't want us to know how bad things were for him because he was so embarrassed, and was afraid we would disown him. That statement alone hurt me so badly. I could never disown a child that wants to be helped, no matter how bad it was.

In the pages above, where Aaron mentions about a girl after high school and the extreme usage of cocaine . . . we remember that girl. We did not know about the cocaine at the time he was dating her. That information came to us at a later date. Although I do remember telling Aaron that she was a strange girl, and we didn't care for her the moment we met her.

I recall being in the yard, deadheading my flowers. He brought her over to introduce her to me and she was almost freaked when she saw what I was doing; these were her words: "Oh, don't pull those flowers off, you're hurting them!" Something was off, but he continued to date her. We were told later that she was the one that got him hooked on the cocaine. That answered the question of why she was so strange.

STATISTICS

Statistics British Columbia

<u>All yellow highlights refer to my son Aaron.</u>

Fentanyl-Detected Illicit Drug Overdose Deaths **January 1, 2012, to September 30, 2017**.

This is the Coroners Service Report of British Columbia, which summarizes all deaths that occurred between January 1, 2012, and September 30, 2017, for which fentanyl was detected, whether alone or in combination with other drugs, and the death resulted from illicit drug use. In the majority of deaths, fentanyl was detected in combination with other drugs.

*   There were 914 illicit drug overdose deaths with fentanyl detected from Jan through Sept 2017. This is a 147% increase over the number of fentanyl detected deaths (370) occurring during the same period in 2016.

*   From Jan to Sept 2017, fentanyl was detected in approximately 83% of illicit drug overdose deaths.

* Carfentanil has been detected in 37 suspected illicit drug overdose deaths in June - Sept 2017. Note this is subject to change as further toxicology results are received.

* Approximately 29% of those dying from Jan - Sept 2017 with fentanyl detected were aged 30 - 39, with 92% between 19 and 59. Males accounted for 83% of all deaths during this period.

* Fraser Health Authority had the highest number (295) of illicit drug overdose deaths with fentanyl from Jan - Sept 2017, followed by Vancouver Coastal Health (269) and Vancouver Island Health Authority (155).

* The Health Service Delivery Areas with the most fentanyl-detected illicit drug overdose deaths from Jan through Sept 2017 were Vancouver (223) Fraser South (146) and Okanagan (100). When looking at individual townships over the same time period, the highest numbers of deaths were seen in Vancouver, Surry and Victoria.

Preliminary data for January through September 2017 suggest that the proportion of apparent illicit drug overdose deaths with fentanyl detected (alone or in combination with other drugs) is approximately 83%.

2012   4 %

2013   15%

2014   25%

2015   29%

2016   68%

2017   (Jan-Sept) 83%

Aaron's death was caused by a combination of fentanyl and a sleeping pill.

Fentanyl-Detected Deaths by Month, 2012-2017[3]						
Month	2012	2013	2014	2015	2016	2017
January	0	5	5	20	46	107
February	0	3	5	8	29	104
March	0	6	9	8	48	115
April	1	8	8	12	48	123
May	1	3	8	8	37	107
June	1	2	6	11	42	100
July	0	1	3	14	40	96
August	1	4	8	15	38	100
September	1	2	9	15	42	62
Subtotal	5	34	61	111	370	914
October	0	4	13	16	53	
November	4	6	6	12	110	
December	3	6	11	13	133	
Total	12	50	91	152	666	914

Fentanyl-Detected Deaths by Sex, 2012-2017[3]							
Sex	2012	2013	2014	2015	2016	2017	Total
Female	2	9	21	26	126	156	340
Male	10	41	70	126	540	758	1,545
Total	12	50	91	152	666	914	1,885

Fentanyl-Detected Deaths by Age Group, 2012-2017[3]							
Age Group	2012	2013	2014	2015	2016	2017	Total
10-18	0	1	0	2	12	10	25
19-29	3	19	28	43	152	176	421
30-39	2	10	33	45	197	266	553
40-49	6	13	19	29	154	214	435
50-59	1	5	7	24	120	183	340
60+	0	2	4	9	31	65	111
Total	12	50	91	152	666	914	1,885

Fentanyl-Detected Deaths by Health Authority of Injury, 2012-2017[3],[5]

HA	2012	2013	2014	2015	2016	2017	Total
Interior	2	3	9	21	116	153	304
Fraser	7	16	29	57	209	295	613
Vancouver Coastal	1	10	26	40	183	269	529
Vancouver Island	1	14	17	22	122	155	331
Northern	1	7	10	12	36	42	108
Total	12	50	91	152	666	914	1,885

Fentanyl-Detected Deaths by Health Service Delivery Area of Injury, 2012-2017[3],[5]

HSDA	2012	2013	2014	2015	2016	2017	Total
East Kootenay	0	1	2	1	6	4	14
Kootenay Boundary	0	0	1	2	4	10	17
Okanagan	2	1	4	14	61	100	182
Thompson Cariboo Shuswap	0	1	2	4	45	39	91
Fraser East	1	3	1	10	37	66	118
Fraser North	1	6	15	28	71	83	204
Fraser South	5	7	13	19	101	146	291
Richmond	0	0	0	3	13	18	34
Vancouver	1	5	22	32	153	223	436
North Shore/Coast Garibaldi	0	5	4	5	17	28	59
South Vancouver Island	1	3	2	9	59	69	143
Central Vancouver Island	0	10	13	10	46	63	142
North Vancouver Island	0	1	2	3	17	23	46
Northwest	0	1	0	1	7	4	13
Northern Interior	1	3	4	7	14	27	56
Northeast	0	3	6	4	15	11	39
Total	12	50	91	152	666	914	1,885

42

Fentanyl-Detected Deaths by Month of Death and Health Authority of Injury, 2017[3],[5]						
HA	Interior	Fraser	Vancouver Coastal	Vancouver Island	Northern	Total
January	13	34	41	18	1	107
February	17	30	30	22	5	104
March	17	38	31	23	6	115
April	17	38	45	18	5	123
May	20	42	27	11	7	107
June	20	29	26	22	3	100
July	22	32	24	14	4	96
August	21	31	24	16	8	100
September	6	21	21	11	3	62
Total	153	295	269	155	42	914

Fentanyl-Detected Deaths by Top Townships of Injury, 2012-2017[3],[5]							
Township	2012	2013	2014	2015	2016	2017	Total
Vancouver	1	5	22	32	153	223	436
Surrey	3	4	8	11	73	108	207
Victoria	0	3	2	8	53	62	128
Kelowna	0	0	1	6	38	56	101
Nanaimo	0	8	12	9	27	33	89
Burnaby	0	3	0	6	27	29	65
Abbotsford	0	1	1	6	22	29	59
Kamloops	0	1	2	3	30	25	61
Langley	1	1	5	6	20	25	58
Maple Ridge	0	3	7	12	20	20	62
Other Township	7	21	31	53	203	304	619
Total	12	50	91	152	666	914	1,885

*sorted by 2017 data

43

Summary

* There were 80 suspected drug deaths in September 2017. This is a 31% increase over the number of deaths occurring in September 2016 (61).

* The number of illicit drug overdose deaths in September 2017 (80) equates to about 2.7 deaths per day for the month.

* In 2017, individuals aged 19–59 accounted for 91% of illicit drug overdose deaths. Males accounted for 83% of all suspected illicit drug overdose deaths in the same period.

* The three townships experiencing the highest number of illicit drug overdoses in 2017 to date are Vancouver, Surrey, and Victoria.

* Fraser and Vancouver Coastal Health Authority have had the highest number of illicit drug overdose deaths (364 and 334 deaths, respectively) to date in 2017, making up 63% of all illicit drug overdose deaths during this period.

* Vancouver Coastal Health Authority has the highest rate of illicit drug overdose

deaths (37.8 deaths per 100,000 individuals), and also experienced the largest increase in rate from 2016 (59% increase) among all the health authorities.

Overall, the rate of illicit drug overdose deaths in BC increased 49% to 30.6 deaths per 100,000 individuals from the 2016 year-end rate of 20.6 deaths per 100,000 individuals.

* Rates of illicit drug overdose deaths are highest in Vancouver, Okanagan, Fraser East, Central Vancouver Island, and North Vancouver Island Health Services Delivery Areas.

* All health authorities saw a decline in the number of illicit drug overdose deaths in September 2017 compared to August 2017.

* 88.1% of illicit drug overdose deaths occurred inside (58.5% private residences, 29.6% other inside locations) and 11.4% occurred outside in vehicles, sidewalks, streets, parks, etc.

* There were no deaths at supervised consumption or drug overdose prevention sites.

- This figure illustrates the comparison of illicit drug overdose deaths to other common causes of unnatural deaths in 2016.

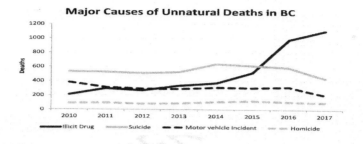

A review of completed cases from 2016–2017 indicates that the top four detected drugs relevant to illicit drug overdose deaths were fentanyl (64.1%), cocaine (47.5%), heroin (33.3 %), and methamphetamine/amphetamine (32.4%).

BC Data by place of death

	2016	2017
Inside:		
Private Residence	606 (61.8%)	645 (58.5%)
Other Residence	228 (23.2%)	282 (25.6%)
Other Inside	40 (4.1%)	45 (4.1%)
Outside	98 (10.0%)	126 (11.4%)
Unknown	9 (0.9%)	5 (0.5%)
TOTAL	**981**	**1,103**

Now I don't know about you, but these stats tell me that the majority of the deaths were from individuals who were recreational users and/or lived at home. Which again makes me suspect that the majority were drugs that were laced with fentanyl, consumed by unsuspecting users.

BC Data and Rates

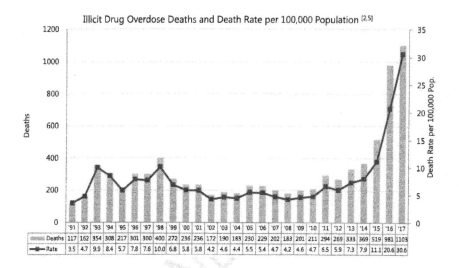

Illicit Drug Overdose Deaths and Death Rate per 100,000 Population [2,5]

	'91	'92	'93	'94	'95	'96	'97	'98	'99	'00	'01	'02	'03	'04	'05	'06	'07	'08	'09	'10	'11	'12	'13	'14	'15	'16	'17
Deaths	117	162	354	308	217	301	300	400	272	236	236	172	190	183	230	229	202	183	201	211	294	269	333	369	519	981	1103
Rate	3.5	4.7	9.9	8.4	5.7	7.8	7.6	10.0	6.8	5.8	5.8	4.2	4.6	4.4	5.5	5.4	4.7	4.2	4.6	4.7	6.5	5.9	7.3	7.9	11.1	20.6	30.6

Illicit Drug Overdose Deaths by Month, British Columbia, 2007-2017[2]

Month	2007	2008	2009	2010	2011	2012	2013	2014	2015	2016	2017
Jan	15	18	23	16	24	20	20	23	42	86	141
Feb	14	8	15	14	24	17	21	39	31	58	118
Mar	19	17	10	15	25	25	33	28	31	77	130
Apr	24	18	8	9	26	31	31	29	34	71	151
May	10	18	19	22	22	19	28	40	41	50	137
Jun	18	18	16	21	22	25	25	29	34	70	119
Jul	11	24	19	23	33	29	38	25	37	71	108
Aug	21	16	27	24	22	19	21	37	52	63	119
Sep	14	12	16	20	22	16	28	31	47	61	80
Subtotal	146	149	153	164	220	201	245	281	349	607	1,103
Oct	15	10	13	18	23	19	19	35	53	74	-
Nov	19	9	18	18	27	28	31	28	49	138	-
Dec	22	15	17	11	24	21	38	25	68	162	-
Total	202	183	201	211	294	269	333	369	519	981	1,103
Average	16.8	15.3	16.8	17.6	24.5	22.4	27.8	30.8	43.3	81.8	122.6

BC Data by Gender/Age:

Illicit Drug Overdose Deaths by Gender, 2007-2017[2]

Gender	2007	2008	2009	2010	2011	2012	2013	2014	2015	2016	2017
Female	47	49	55	49	82	75	79	86	102	193	192
Male	155	134	146	162	212	194	254	283	417	788	911
Total	202	183	201	211	294	269	333	369	519	981	1103

Illicit Drug Overdose Deaths by Age Group, 2007-2017[2]

Age Group	2007	2008	2009	2010	2011	2012	2013	2014	2015	2016	2017
10-18	5	6	2	4	4	5	6	3	5	12	16
19-29	33	36	46	40	74	61	94	83	118	206	205
30-39	53	48	51	49	75	61	77	101	135	261	311
40-49	70	42	57	66	77	66	74	85	126	231	269
50-59	36	43	33	45	54	56	61	72	108	222	219
60-69	4	8	12	7	10	19	21	25	26	46	77
70-79	1	0	0	0	0	1	0	0	1	3	6
Total	202	183	201	211	294	269	333	369	519	981	1103

Note: The age range of decedents of illicit drug overdose between 2007-2017 ranged from 13 to 76 years of age.

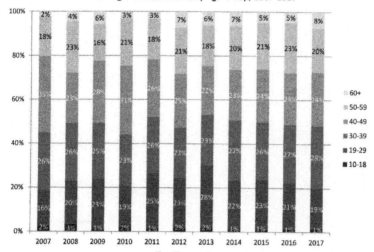

Illicit Drug Overdose Deaths by Age Group, 2007-2017

Age-Specific Illicit Drug Overdose Death Rates per 100,000, 2007-2017[5,7]										
Age Group	2007	2008	2009	2010	2011	2012	2013	2014	2015	2016	2017
10-18	1.0	1.3	0.4	0.9	0.9	1.1	1.3	0.7	1.1	2.7	4.8
19-29	5.2	5.5	6.9	5.9	10.9	8.9	13.7	11.9	16.8	29.2	38.7
30-39	9.1	8.2	8.6	8.3	12.6	10.1	12.6	16.2	21.4	40.7	63.4
40-49	10.1	6.1	8.3	9.7	11.4	9.9	11.3	13.2	19.8	36.5	56.6
50-59	5.8	6.8	5.1	6.8	8.0	8.2	8.8	10.3	15.3	31.6	41.8
60-69	1.0	1.8	2.6	1.5	2.0	3.7	3.9	4.5	4.5	7.7	16.8
70-79	0.4	0.0	0.0	0.0	0.0	0.3	0.0	0.0	0.3	0.9	2.1
Total	4.7	4.2	4.6	4.7	6.5	5.9	7.3	7.9	11.1	20.6	30.6

51

BC Data by Township of Injury:

Illicit Drug Overdose Deaths by Top Townships of Injury, 2007-2017* [2,4]											
Township	2007	2008	2009	2010	2011	2012	2013	2014	2015	2016	2017
Vancouver	59	38	60	42	69	65	80	101	136	232	281
Surrey	22	20	23	33	42	44	36	44	76	121	133
Victoria	19	29	13	13	17	17	25	20	21	67	70
Kelowna	6	2	5	9	14	8	12	12	19	47	63
Nanaimo	2	2	6	4	8	6	20	16	19	28	38
Burnaby	9	12	8	9	10	10	13	12	16	39	35
Abbotsford	3	4	4	10	16	7	10	7	26	39	35
Kamloops	11	7	7	10	2	5	8	7	7	43	33
Langley	3	6	2	3	10	5	10	10	10	31	28
Maple Ridge	5	2	6	4	4	5	10	14	29	27	26
Chilliwack	3	4	2	2	8	8	6	6	10	12	21
Coquitlam	2	2	5	2	3	6	1	10	11	13	21
Richmond	0	1	3	4	4	1	3	3	6	14	19
Prince George	5	2	4	1	6	10	7	10	12	18	18
Vernon	3	1	4	6	7	1	11	6	8	12	17
Other Township	50	51	49	59	74	71	81	91	113	238	265
Total	202	183	201	211	294	269	333	369	519	981	1103

*sorted by 2017 totals

BC Data by Day of Week:

Illicit Drug Overdose Deaths by Day of Week of Injury, British Columbia, 2007-2017[2,3]											
Day	2007	2008	2009	2010	2011	2012	2013	2014	2015	2016	2017
Monday	25	21	15	29	39	32	33	38	68	102	129
Tuesday	23	24	24	26	27	35	42	37	63	118	126
Wednesday	24	25	31	30	35	37	36	49	68	129	156
Thursday	24	25	27	33	51	34	41	60	73	151	161
Friday	38	31	28	33	42	32	57	60	77	137	192
Saturday	34	34	34	35	53	46	72	72	88	181	172
Sunday	34	23	42	25	47	53	52	53	82	163	167
Total	202	183	201	211	294	269	333	369	519	981	1103

Illicit Drug Overdose Deaths by Month of Death and Health Authority and Township, 2016-2017[4,6,8]							
		Health Authorities				Township	
Year	Month	Interior	Fraser	Vancouver Coastal	Vancouver Island	Northern	Vancouver	Surrey
2016	Jan	17	28	22	15	4	19	10
	Feb	10	20	16	10	2	14	8
	Mar	12	30	12	15	8	11	9
	Apr	9	24	15	15	8	10	8
	May	10	21	7	8	4	5	9
	Jun	10	29	20	7	4	17	10
	Jul	9	25	18	16	3	13	13
	Aug	6	23	22	10	2	20	8
	Sep	13	19	14	12	3	13	8
	Oct	15	18	24	15	2	17	6
	Nov	20	47	52	18	1	44	15
	Dec	31	49	55	17	10	49	17
2017	Jan	20	46	54	20	1	49	13
	Feb	18	36	35	24	5	32	15
	Mar	22	42	36	24	6	27	13
	Apr	19	49	56	21	6	45	12
	May	26	55	37	12	7	31	21
	Jun	21	36	35	23	4	28	13
	Jul	25	36	28	15	4	24	17
	Aug	25	37	28	20	9	22	18
	Sep	9	27	25	16	3	23	11
Total		347	697	611	333	96	513	254
Average		16.5	33.2	29.1	15.9	4.6	24.4	12.1

Illicit Drug Overdose Deaths by Health Services Delivery Area, 2007-2017[2,4,6]											
HSDA	2007	2008	2009	2010	2011	2012	2013	2014	2015	2016	2017
East Kootenay	2	2	1	0	1	2	4	4	2	13	6
Kootenay Boundary	4	0	2	3	4	4	2	3	6	9	13
Okanagan	13	9	15	18	28	16	33	27	42	76	118
Thompson Cariboo	16	11	17	16	5	9	15	13	13	64	48
Fraser East	9	14	9	22	31	20	20	16	41	67	79
Fraser North	19	22	23	26	25	30	35	52	74	102	109
Fraser South	29	29	26	38	59	54	51	59	93	164	176
Richmond	0	1	3	4	4	1	3	3	6	14	19
Vancouver	59	38	60	42	69	65	80	101	136	232	281
North Shore/Coast Garibaldi	5	8	6	6	8	6	12	15	15	31	34
South Vancouver Island	21	31	15	13	17	20	26	23	25	76	77
Central Vancouver Island	8	6	13	6	17	20	24	25	30	55	71
North Vancouver Island	6	6	5	4	10	4	9	7	11	27	27
Northwest	2	2	0	3	1	0	6	2	6	11	5
Northern Interior	7	3	5	7	8	12	8	11	15	23	27
Northeast	2	1	1	3	7	6	5	8	4	17	13
Total	202	183	201	211	294	269	333	369	519	981	1,103

BC Data by Relevant Drugs Detected:

Top Relevant Drugs Detected Among Illicit Drug Overdose Deaths, 2016-17	
Drug Detected	BC (n=510)
Fentanyl	64.1%
Cocaine	47.5%
Heroin	33.3%
Meth/amph	32.4%
Ethyl alcohol	25.3%
Other opioids	19.4%
Methadone	8.6%
Other drugs	19.0%

Note: Relevant drugs are drugs noted by the coroner as being relevant to the death (this data is only available for concluded investigations). As deaths could involve multiple drugs, percentages can add up to more than 100%. Meth/amph includes methamphetamine and amphetamine. Other opioids include codeine, oxycodone, morphine, hydromorphine etc but excludes heroin, fentanyl, fentanyl analogues, and methadone. Other drug includes benzodiazepines & Z-drugs, antidepressants, antiepileptics, antipsychotics, MDMA/MDA, cannabinoids, over-the-counter drugs, and other drugs not listed.

Top Relevant Drugs Detected Among Illicit Drug Overdose Deaths, 2016-2017

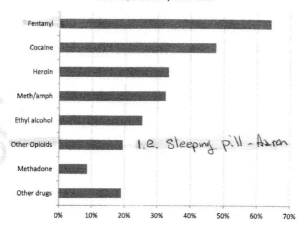

i.e. Sleeping pill - Aaron

55

Statistics Canada

Fentanyl has contributed to the deaths of several Canadians every day in 2017, according to statistics from various provincial agencies.

The drug is disproportionately harming people in Western Canada, according to statistics, but because provinces vary in how they record deaths, it's difficult to come up with a full national picture.

Nonetheless, even without knowing all the details of fentanyl's impact in every province, it's safe to say that it plays a role in the deaths of more than four people on average every day in British Columbia and Alberta alone.

Here's what we know:
British Columbia
Fentanyl was associated with 368 overdose deaths in British Columbia between January and April 2017, according to a

report from the BC Coroners Service. That is a 115 percent increase over the same period in 2016.

In the majority of these deaths, fentanyl was detected along with other drugs. Moreover, this doesn't include cases where the fentanyl was prescribed or the death was due to intentional self-harm. Men accounted for 82 percent of deaths.

Fentanyl was detected in approximately 72 percent of apparent drug overdose deaths in British Columbia so far this year. This is a higher percentage than ever before. In 2014, it was only found in 25 percent of overdose deaths.

Alberta

Fentanyl was implicated in 176 overdose deaths in Alberta between January 1 and May 13, 2017. The more potent related drug, carfentanil, was detected in 34 of those deaths, according to data from Alberta Health.

This year is already shaping up to be worse than last year in the province. Between January and March 2016, there were 70 fentanyl-related deaths. In that same period in 2017, there were 120. *(Global News.ca 2017 BC Coroners service)*

Saskatchewan

There has only been one confirmed fentanyl-related death in Saskatchewan so far this year, according to a report released by the provincial coroner. However, unlike coroners in British Columbia and some other provinces, Saskatchewan only seems to release data when the death has been fully investigated, which can take years.

The coroner's data report mentions that data from 2015, 2016, and 2017 are still subject to change. In 2015, there were 22 fentanyl-related deaths. In 2016, there were seven confirmed so far.

Other opioid drugs, like hydromorphone and methadone, seem to have contributed to more deaths in this province than fentanyl.

Manitoba

Manitoba, like some other provinces, only releases finalized data on causes of death. So, it only has partial figures from 2016 available so far, according to the office of the medical examiner. Among cases the office has closed, fentanyl was identified 10 times as being the primary cause of death. It was identified as a "contributing factor"—meaning that it appeared in a toxicity screening—in an additional 7 cases, for a total of 17 fentanyl-related deaths.

The office is still reviewing 2016 deaths, so these numbers will likely change.

Ontario

Ontario currently only has full data available for 2015. The province has not yet published full 2016 totals or anything from 2017, meaning it's hard to get a current picture of overdose deaths in the province.

But in 2015, fentanyl was implicated in 220 deaths in the province, or about 30 percent of all opioid-related deaths. In the first six months of 2016, there were 76 confirmed deaths related to opioids. There is no data available on the government's website about which drugs specifically were involved in these 2016 deaths, and that number can be expected to change as the coroner investigates and confirms more cases.

Quebec

The most recent stats from Quebec are from 2015, when the province recorded 30 deaths related to accidental overdoses of fentanyl, alone or combined with other drugs.

The provincial coroner's office notes that it takes on average of 10.5 months for an investigation to be completed, so these numbers may still change.

Thirty fentanyl-related deaths in 2015 was a significant jump; there were only eleven the year before.

New Brunswick

Between January and March 2017, only one death was associated with fentanyl in New Brunswick, out of two opioid-related deaths. There were three fentanyl-related deaths in 2016.

Prince Edward Island

PEI had one fentanyl-related death in both 2014 and 2015, and none in 2016, though there are still a handful of cases pending investigation, according to a government spokesperson.

There were three confirmed opioid-related deaths and two cases pending in 2016. There is no readily available data from 2017.

Nova Scotia

As of June 30, 2017, there was one death caused by fentanyl in the province this year, according to Nova Scotia's chief medical examiner's office. There were 24 confirmed and 5 probable opioid deaths.

Provincial documents recently obtained by Global News through an access to information request showed that there were eight fentanyl-related deaths in 2016.

Newfoundland and Labrador

The province did not return an inquiry by deadline, but according to a recent report by the Canadian press, there were 20 drug-related accidental deaths in 2015. Eighteen of those were related to opioids, and five were related to fentanyl.

So the question now is, why are fentanyl-related deaths higher in Western Canada than anywhere else in Canada?

———————————

Alan says he is based in the southern metropolis of Guangzhou, the trading crossroads for manufacturing in China—a country that is, in turn, at the centre of the vast underground world of synthetic drug manufacturers. Enforcement is fragmented, and companies operate with impunity.

Fentanyl is an opioid, a class of painkillers that also includes oxycodone and morphine. Prescription-grade fentanyl is up to 100 times more toxic than morphine. Developed in 1959 by a Belgian chemist, it was quickly adopted as a pain reliever and anesthetic in medical settings. It came into widespread use in the mid-1990s, with the introduction of the transdermal patch that releases the drug into the patient's bloodstream over two or three days. When the drug is processed in a clandestine lab with no quality controls, it is difficult to get the dosage right, making it potentially much more dangerous.

Chemical companies in China custom-design variants of pharmaceutical-grade fentanyl by tweaking a molecule ever so slightly. A few hundred micrograms—the weight of a single grain of salt—are enough to trigger heroin-like bliss. But the line between euphoria and fatal overdose is frighteningly thin: an amount the size of two grains of salt can kill a healthy adult.

The supply chain for illicit fentanyl begins in China, but the problems Canada is experiencing start right here at home. No other country in the world consumes more prescription opioids on a per-capita basis, according to a recent United Nations report. The widespread use of prescription opioids is behind the rise of a new class of drug addicts, many of who are turning to the black market to feed their habit. In British Columbia and Alberta, the two hardest-hit provinces, fatal overdoses linked to fentanyl soared from 42 in 2012 to 418 in 2015.

The supplier, who identified himself only as Alan, says he has two customers in Canada. He emails photos of fentanyl hidden inside silica desiccant packets—the type normally used when shipping goods such as electronics—and a screenshot of a recent order from Canada including a shipping address for a clothing store in British Columbia's picturesque Okanagan Valley. Suppliers in China hide fentanyl in decoy packages before shipping the drug to Canada. Sometimes they conceal the drug alongside urine test strips, as shown below.

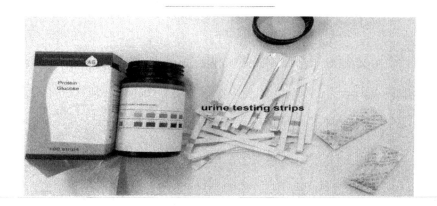

Little is known about the companies in China that make fentanyl, including whether the substance is the product of backyard laboratories or professional chemists concocting it on the side. Or, more likely, both.

As long as Chinese officials do not crack down more aggressively on exporters, medical experts say, the responsibility for change falls squarely on those in power at the end of the supply chain. "It's a national tragedy," says Meldon Kahan, medical director of the Substance Use Service at Women's College Hospital in Toronto, "and a health-care tragedy where most groups don't come out looking very good." *(Globe and Mail.com Article 29570025, 2017)*

Take a look at the next map: direct shipping from China to the West Coast.
(Globe and mail 2017)

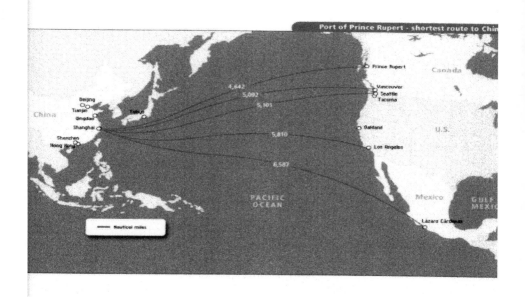

Police across Canada have shut down 20 fentanyl labs since that first major bust in April 2013, mostly operated by organized crime groups, according to a *Globe review*. The biggest raids were in British Columbia, Alberta, and Saskatchewan. Police have also made dozens of busts involving illicit fentanyl and the prescription-grade patches. This week, police charged a doctor and a pharmacist from the Toronto area with participating in a fentanyl trafficking ring. (This was November 21, 2017.)

Below is a map of number of fentanyl lab busts.

(Globe and mail 2017)

Because illicit fentanyl and fentanyl analogues are so potent, the white powder is cut or mixed with other drugs and fillers before it can be sold on the street. Most of the 21 clandestine labs dismantled by police since 2013 operated in British Columbia and Alberta, according to a *Globe and Mail* analysis.

Once processed, the drug is moved to large cities, such as Calgary. Fentanyl is often transported in vehicles outfitted with customized hidden compartments. Calgary is a key destination because as well as having a large population, it serves as the drug gateway to southern Alberta, including the hard-hit community of Blood Tribe. Illicit opioid use is higher in the city compared with the provincial average.

Traffickers range from organized crime to lone operators; Organized crime groups engaged in drug cartels, including the Hells Angels, are involved in trafficking, as well as individuals ordering fentanyl from their homes over the internet. In Calgary, police are investigating so-called nominees—people paid to accept packages from a courier at their home or business on behalf of drug traffickers.

Juurlink, who is on a steering committee to change the guidelines for prescribing opioids in Canada, says a massive increase in prescriptions for narcotic painkillers that started 20 years ago paved the way for today's fentanyl and carfentanil crisis. *(Dr. David Juurlink Canadian pharmacologist & internal Medicine: University of Toronto)*

Opioids, including morphine, OxyContin, and fentanyl, work by binding the receptors on cells in the brain and spinal cord, blocking the perception of pain. But up until the mid-1990s, Juurlink said, they were usually prescribed only for acute pain, such as broken bones, pain caused by cancer, or for palliative care.

That attitude changed when medical students and doctors were told that opioids could also be used to treat chronic pain, and that the risk of addiction for their patients was low.

But by the mid-2000s, when medication like OxyContin was being widely prescribed, it became clear that many chronic pain patients were on a "spiral into addiction." *(Dr. David Juurlink:*

Steering committee to change the guidelines for prescribing opioids in Canada, www.cbc.ca/news/health 2017)

The sheer amount of painkillers being prescribed also "put a lot of opioids into medicine cabinets that otherwise wouldn't have been there," Juurlink said, which in turn led to teens experimenting with their parents' drugs, and "millions" of tablets falling into the wrong hands. *(Dr. David Juurlink: Steering committee to change the guidelines for prescribing opioids in Canada, www.cbc.ca/news/health 2017)*

When the medical community started to recognize the damage being done, the culture of prescribing opioids began to shift, and many doctors stopped giving them to their chronic pain patients.

But making pharmaceutical opioids less available didn't change the fact that thousands of people were addicted to them—and the withdrawal symptoms were unbearable. Imagine the worst flu you've ever had, multiply it by 20, and you are miserable.

The "sheer enormity of the market" of people addicted to opioids has led drug dealers to maximize their heroin supplies as much as they can, Juurlink said, and that's where fentanyl—and more recently, carfentanil—comes in. *(www.cbc.ca/news/health/fentanyl 2017)*

Fentanyl is cheap and "incredibly potent," so drug dealers add it to heroin to multiply the effects and increase their profits, he said. But because "quality control isn't exactly their thing," how much fentanyl they add varies widely, and even a tiny bit too much kills.

People using street drugs "literally have no clue what they're getting," Juurlink said. *(www.cbc.ca/news/health/fentanyl 2017)*

But what alarms him even more than fentanyl is the recently discovered presence of carfentanil, which was never intended to be consumed by humans, in other drugs.

Carfentanil, also an opioid, is chemically related to fentanyl, but is 100 times more potent and used in veterinary medicine to sedate large animals.

It's "one of the most frightening drugs I can imagine in circulation," said Juurlink. "It's only a matter of time before it is detected in every province in Canada."
(www.cbc.ca/news/health/fentanyl-carfentanil 2017

Both fentanyl and carfentanil pose enormous danger not only to people with addictions, he said, but also to anyone—including kids—who might try a pill or drug at a party that isn't what they think it is.
"This happens. And those people fall asleep and they stop breathing and they die."

How can those deaths be prevented?

Experts, including Juurlink, are calling on the Canadian government to support safe consumption sites, where people suffering from addiction are supervised and can be resuscitated if the drug they take is contaminated with fentanyl or carfentanil. In addition, those sites can provide a gateway to addiction counselling and anti-withdrawal drugs that can help someone stop using illicit substances.

Statistics US

According to the National Center for Health Statistics, estimates for the first nine months of 2016 were higher than the first nine months of the previous year, which had already reached an all-time high of 53,404 deaths by overdose. Of those, more than 33,000 were attributed to opioid drugs, including legal prescription painkillers, as well as illicit drugs like heroin and street fentanyl.

Provisional Counts of Drug Overdose Deaths, as of 8/6/2017

Selected Jurisdictions	Drug overdose deaths			Data quality	
	Number of deaths for 12 month-ending			12 month-ending Jan-2017	
	Jan-2016	Jan-2017	% Change	% Complete	% Pending investigation
US Total	52,898	64,070	21	99+	0.25
22 Reporting Jurisdictions	21,061	26,841	27	100	0.07
Alaska	126	126	0	100	0.09
Arkansas	378	382	1	100	0.08
Colorado	913	970	6	100	0.05
Delaware	181	309	71	100	0.01
Florida	3,324	5,167	55	100	0.06
Georgia	1,299	1,366	5	100	0.10
Illinois	1,893	2,518	33	100	0.04
Indiana	1,228	1,566	28	100	0.02
Iowa	303	324	7	99+	0.00
Kentucky	1,253	1,480	18	100	0.01
Louisiana	890	1,015	14	100	0.01
Maine	270	359	33	100	0.11
Maryland	1,303	2,171	67	100	0.04
Minnesota	607	655	8	100	0.00
Missouri	1,096	1,384	26	100	0.02
Nebraska	122	112	-8	100	0.04
New York City	987	1,478	50	100	0.08
North Dakota	62	80	29	99+	0.28
Texas	2,593	2,799	8	100	0.18
Virginia	1,005	1,387	38	100	0.02
Washington	1,134	1,102	-3	100	0.04
Wyoming	94	91	-3	100	0.00

(CDC. National Center for Health Statistics 2017)

PROVISIONAL COUNTS OF DRUG OVERDOSE DEATHS, as of 8/6/2017

Provisional counts for 2016 and 2017 are based on data available for analysis as of the date specified. Provisional counts should be interpreted with caution and in the context of the data quality. Provisional counts may be incomplete and causes of death may be pending investigation. Reporting of specific drugs and drug classes varies by jurisdiction and estimates should be interpreted with caution. Deaths are reported by the jurisdiction in which the death occurred.

Drug overdose deaths involving specific drugs and drug classes, United States and 7 Jurisdictions, 12 month-ending Jan 2016, Jan 2017

Drug Type	United States		Alaska		Iowa		Maine		Maryland		New York City		Virginia		Washington	
	Number of deaths for 12 month-ending															
	Jan-16	Jan-17	Jan-16	Jan-17	Jan-16	Jan-17	Jan-16	Jan-17	Jan-16	Jan-17	Jan-16	Jan-17	Jan-16	Jan-17	Jan-16	Jan-17
Heroin (T40.1)	13,219	15,446	35	50	40	52	49	54	418	679	421	595	339	451	323	285
Natural and semi-synthetic opioids (T40.2)	12,726	14,427	60	40	76	87	108	131	394	712	222	337	270	346	272	281
Methadone (T40.3)	3,276	3,314	13	11	22	15	34	38	179	200	125	177	73	70	119	127
Synthetic opioids excluding methadone (T40.4)	9,945	20,145	13	10	47	61	111	208	386	1,222	154	628	263	692	81	101
Cocaine (T40.5)	6,986	10,619	9	15	17	18	32	58	154	328	308	537	168	263	86	82
Psychostimulants with abuse potential (T43.6)	5,922	7,663	27	55	61	81	23	31	21	48	49	60	45	68	316	338
Quality: % of overdose deaths with drug(s) specified	83%	85%	90%	99%	90%	93%	99%	99%	99%	99%	98%	100%	98%	99%	95%	93%

NOTES ON DATA QUALITY: Provisional counts for 12 months-ending are the number of deaths received and processed for the 12 month period ending in the month indicated. Deaths are classified by reporting jurisdiction in which the death occurred. Jurisdictions are selected for inclusion in the report based on two measures of data quality: 1) overall completeness of reporting (≥ 90%); 2) percentage of records pending investigation (≤ 1.2%); and for reporting deaths involving specific drugs and drug classes, 3) percentage of overdose deaths with drug specified (≥ 92%). Drug overdose deaths are identified using ICD-10 underlying cause-of-death codes X40–X44, X60–X64, X85, and Y10–Y14. Drug overdose deaths involving selected drug categories are identified by ICD-10 multiple-cause-of-death codes (MCOD): heroin, T40.1; natural and semisynthetic opioids, T40.2; methadone, T40.3; synthetic opioids excluding methadone, T40.4; cocaine, T40.5; and psychostimulants with abuse potential, T43.6. Categories are not mutually exclusive because deaths may involve more than one drug. Among deaths with an underlying cause of drug overdose, the percent with at least one drug or drug class specified were identified through MCODs in the range T36–T50.8.

CDC • National Center for Health Statistics • National Vital Statistics System

US HEROIN DEATHS JUMP 533% SINCE 2002, REPORT SAYS. **(CNN)** - The number of heroin users in the United States jumped from 404,000 in 2002 to 948,000 in 2016, a 135% increase, according to the most recent government numbers. But even more striking: The number of people who had fatal overdoses related to heroin has skyrocketed from 2,089 in 2002 to an estimated 13,219 in 2016 - a 533% jump.

These numbers are a striking marker of the lethality of the opioid epidemic that has taken root across the country.

Fentanyl is a major factor in rising overdose deaths. More American lives are lost to drugs than were lost in Vietnam, an official says. *(cnn.com 2017/9/8 health/heroin)*

This year, drug overdose deaths are expected to reach an all-time high of 71,600. *(Dr, Tom Price: Health and Human services secretary - cnn.com health/heroin 2017/9/8)*

According to the US Centers for Disease Control and Prevention, drug overdoses are the leading cause of accidental death in America, killing more people than guns or car accidents. *(cnn.com 2017/9/8 - health/heroin, CDC)*

It's a trend that doesn't appear to be reversing course. The CDC estimates that there were more than 52,000 overdose deaths for 2016, and projects that number to climb 38% to over 71,000 in 2017. Opioids continue to be the drivers for these overdoses, including legally prescribed prescription painkillers, as well as illegal drugs. In fact, the number of overdose deaths related to merely fentanyl is expected to more than double, from an estimated 9,945 in 2016 to 20,145 in 2017, the CDC says. *(cnn.com 2017/9/8)*

The CDC is also seeing a trend in overdose deaths related to cocaine, which have increased steadily from over 4,000 in 2009 to over 6,700 in 2015. The agency expects that number to rise to over 6,900 in 2016 and then to make a 52% jump to almost 11,000 cocaine-related deaths this year. *(cnn.com U S heroin deaths 2017/9/8)*

"These are the highest numbers ever recorded in a single year. A lot of these fatalities are related to fentanyl," Baume said. He emphasized the need to better understand why drug users would use multiple substances. *(Richard Baum: acting director of the White House's office of National Drug Control Policy)*

And while there has been a reported increase in cocaine production, Kolodny said that the rise in cocaine-related overdoses was a logical result of increased fentanyl use. *(Dr. Andrew Kolodny: executive director of physicians for responsible opioid prescribing)*

"As we see more people dying of fentanyl overdoses, you're going to start seeing other things in their system," Kolodny says.

_____

THE OPIATE ADDICTION

Aaron had such a huge heart; he always gave to people, even homeless people. One Christmas, when he was unemployed and didn't have much money himself, he gave $20.00 to a street person that was sitting outside a store. It made him feel so good to give to others, even though he couldn't afford to give the money away. He told me that he at least had a home and family that cared about him, and that was more than the homeless person he gave the $20.00 to.

We were so proud of Aaron in so many ways. He had such a bright future ahead of him. He would have been a success at whatever he did. Aaron would have been a wonderful husband and father. We were so looking forward to having a little Aaron running around.

He had finished his fourth year of Millwright and was in the top 80 to 90% in his class. Unfortunately, when he finished his schooling in 2015, there wasn't anything he could find available for positions. While he was doing his schooling he was working for an oil company in Alberta, and he was a technician servicing the pumps in the oil fields. They would send him to Germany and Egypt. He just loved his job. He would have still been working there if it wasn't for his accident.

In September of 2016, we got a phone call from Aaron's girlfriend, Shauna. She was crying on the phone and explained to us what Aaron was going through with the drugs. She told us that she had taken care of him twice now while he was going through detox, and she just couldn't do it anymore. (Helping someone go through detox is a very difficult thing to deal with, especially when you are not a professional.)

It came as such a shock; we had no idea what he was on and for how long. He had made her promise not to tell us. He was so ashamed that he had become an addict, and didn't want us to know because he thought we would disown him. Obviously, we wish she would have broken her promise earlier and told us, but she loved him so much, she didn't want to break his trust in her.

So, we told him to come home to British Columbia and stay with us as long as need be so we could help him and get him back on track again. When he lost his job in Alberta (he was on disability for about six months, went back to work on light duties, and then they laid him off), it was so devastating to him, because he loved his job. This took a huge toll on Aaron, and I know his drug usage would have gotten worse at that point in time.

———————

Aaron's previous girlfriend, Kristen, told us Aaron told her that the addiction to the painkillers was the beginning of the more serious problem: street drugs. He told her that when the painkillers stopped working, he needed something else, and that's when he turned to the heroin. (Which was introduced to him by a friend who is now also dead; he died approximately a year before Aaron.)

To this day, I have a Ziploc bag full of prescriptions that were prescribed for Aaron from doctors in the Edmonton area. (They shall remain nameless for now). There is one doctor in particular that I feel should have his license revoked. He prescribed Aaron Hydromorphone 8 mg tablets. The street name for this drug is Hillbilly Heroin. He was given 90 tablets, with a refill of 210. This prescription was filled in September 2015, 1 year and 7 months after Aaron's accident, so I can only guess how many before this period were prescribed. Along with that he also prescribed 7.5 mg of zopiclone (30) with two refills, and paroxetine 30 mg (Paxil). Plus, he was on amitriptyline 10 mg for pain.

Well, suffice it to say, Aaron was hooked . . . not surprised! So his doctor cut him off. No help for withdrawals, no counselling, nothing. At that point Aaron started clinic-jumping, until they all caught up with him. Again, no help getting weaned off of these narcotics, just an abrupt door slammed in his face.

Aaron talked to a buddy of his regarding his pain, and of course his buddy steered him in the direction of no return. Heroin. The worst drug anyone could ever inflict upon themselves. My beautiful, naive son, not knowing what he was getting himself into, took advice from someone he only knew a short time, instead of coming to us, his parents. The day he started this was the beginning of the end. To this day we cannot understand WHY IN HELL he would touch one of the worst drugs on this planet.

It's amazing how a child you think you know inside and out can get himself into such deep trouble with drugs and hide it from his/her family and consistently lie about it. That's what Aaron did. I know he was ashamed of what he had gotten himself into. I was told by his girlfriend how he would cry and tell her that he didn't want us to know about the drugs because he was afraid of being disowned. That broke my heart hearing that. Did he not feel he could confide in us? Did he not trust that we would do what was in his best interest? He knew how much we loved him. I know now that it was the drugs that destroyed his thinking; the drugs rewired his brain. He had always come to us whenever he had a problem. He knew either his dad or I would help him solve anything he needed help with. But in Aaron's state of mind, I guess he thought we would shun him. It truly hurts us to know that he felt he could not come to us with this problem until it was too late.

Aaron arrived home in September of 2016. He brought his dog, Axl, a French bulldog mix (adorable pup), and it was about a month later when we told him it was time that he try to get his life back. "Let's start by you getting a job so you can pay your bills and start to feel normal again." I told him, "I have no problem looking after Axl while you're at work," even though we had three dogs of our own.

He got a job framing. He wasn't happy about it, because that's not what he wanted to do. He took it anyway, then a few weeks later, he told us he also took a part-time job at Canadian Tire. We said it was too much. "You're just going to tire your body, and you can't handle that right now," both Jim and I said. But he didn't listen, and worked Monday through Friday at framing, and some of those nights and the weekends at Canadian Tire.

Then he'd come home and tell us he was going to do some house renovations for a friend the other couple of nights. OMG, he was overdoing it!

He would get home from work just bagged, and usually late, like after 8:00 p.m., and most of the times he was not hungry. That seemed odd. He hardly ever ate lunch (at first I made his lunch for him), then I told him that he had to start making his own lunch because he wasn't a child anymore. I think he did make his lunch a few times but that was it.

The not wanting to eat set an alarm off with us. He was working for this framing company for a few months, but he was getting further behind on his bills. We couldn't understand why, because he didn't have to pay rent at home or for his food. He just had a phone bill, truck insurance, and gas. So where was the money going?

I helped him out with a payment structure on the bills he owed, plus paying back some of the approximately $25,000 he owed his girlfriend. He had also owed us in the teens and his credit cards were maxed. We now know the majority of this debt went to the drugs. It was disgusting. The financial debt he was in was so disheartening for him that it pulled him further down into depression. Which went hand in hand with drugs; do the drugs, and you feel like you're on top of the world again. It's a no-win situation.

No one, not us or Shauna, Aaron's girlfriend, pushed for him to pay back the money. We all knew he was in dire straits. We also found out that he had put up most of his possessions that were worth something to a pawn shop. Some of those items we were lucky to get back after he passed away. We of course had to buy them back.

After a month of doing the renovations, he quit because the girl he did the work for wouldn't pay him for what he had already done. He was using his own gas money and our tile cutter and she wouldn't contribute, so he said, enough. We had told him weeks prior if she doesn't pay you something up front, don't do it. Well, he was a sucker (he always trusted everyone, and she was a school friend). I felt really bad for him.

As time passed, we found out that a co-worker Aaron worked with at Canadian Tire would give Aaron pills to help stop his leg pain and help keep him awake. Also, the boss he worked for in construction was selling drugs (i.e., crack, cocaine, etc.). So now that answered a lot of questions as to where Aaron was getting his drugs from and where his money was going.

How pathetic; here is Aaron, trying to help and better himself, and he was being enabled by people he worked with. I hope those people realize that they helped Aaron travel the road of no return! And I hope payback comes their way. He just couldn't get away from the drugs no matter which way he turned. He couldn't even do an honest day's work without someone throwing drugs in his face.

Here are some stats on the most powerful drugs that are causing addiction today, and don't for one minute think that your child is immune from this. That old saying, "It won't happen to my child . . ." If you still think that way, then you had better wake up! Take your blinders off and start snooping in your child's room when they are not around. Look in every nook and cranny. I found a joint once when Aaron was around 15 years old. He had it hidden inside a pen. He took the guts out of the pen and slid the joint in it and then put the pen back together again. We only stumbled across it because we picked it up and shook it (why, I don't know), but I could feel something sliding in it. Very sneaky.

DETOXING - SHAUNA'S STORY

I've asked Aaron's girlfriend, Shauna, to contribute a chapter from her point of view. This is her experience with trying to help Aaron detox.

***

I believe it was November 27, 2015, when Aaron knocked on my door around 9:00 p.m. He had been very distant the previous three weeks—not always answering his phone or wanting to get together like we normally would. I had just bought Aaron a puppy, because he was feeling lonely. He named him Axl, after Axl Rose of Guns and Roses. During the three weeks that he had Axl, he would often ask me to take him to my house for a few nights because he said he wasn't feeling well, which I found was strange, since he was already so in love with his little "Mr. Wiggles."

When I opened the door that night, Aaron fell into my arms crying. He said he had something to tell me but was terrified of losing me once I heard what he had to say. We were planning on moving in together in the next few weeks.

It took Aaron over a half-hour to calm down enough to tell me that he had been addicted to Dilaudid since December 6, 2014. He confessed that he had problems being addicted to Dilaudid from his past leg surgeries and that he had tried to get through the pain this time without Dilaudid for fear of becoming addicted again. He said that the pain was too unbearable, and his doctor once again prescribed him Dilaudid.

Aaron then told me that in August of that year, while doing a month-long training course in Oklahoma, he was running low on Dilaudid so he tried injecting it to conserve what little he had left until he could return to Canada to get a prescription refill. He didn't want to have to deal with the symptoms of withdrawals while he was on his training course.

His confession hit me like a tonne of bricks. And if this wasn't bad enough, he continued to say that his doctor had suddenly cut him off of Dilaudid without telling him, which led him to resort to doing heroin to prevent the withdrawals. He told me that he had tried so hard to get clean on his own but couldn't handle the pain of detoxing, so his friend introduced him to heroin to combat the withdrawals. He said his plan was to keep the withdrawals at bay so he could deal with his addiction by slowly weaning off of heroin. He explained that he had to do this so he could safely detox.

Aaron felt so embarrassed and ashamed. He said he had been trying to get off heroin, but needed my help. The terrified look in his eyes was so incredibly painful to see. I gave him a great big hug and we stayed hugging one another and crying for what felt like an eternity. Aaron was such a loving, caring, happy-go-lucky guy, who had such a passion for life that I knew I had to support him in every way I could, but I was completely out of my league. I had never dealt with drugs or addiction. I had never even taken drugs in my life, so I was completely naive looking at the road that lay ahead.

Once Aaron fell asleep, the whirlwind of information he had just confessed to started to sink in. I was literally sick to my stomach—I spent hours that night in the bathroom going between vomiting, crying, and having panic attacks. I had no idea what to do or how to help Aaron.

That first night, while Aaron tried to sleep, he experienced restlessness, and bounced back and forth between shivering and sweating. I tried to keep him warm and dry but it was impossible. I did some online research on Dilaudid and heroin and looked for detox clinics and other resources in our area. Little did I know, the peak of Aaron's withdrawals would come the next day.

I don't think either of us slept for the next 2 or 3 nights. Aaron was sweating profusely yet freezing to the core. His head and whole body ached right down to his bones. Aaron was extremely restless, and he couldn't stop moving, almost like he was having muscle spasms. Those days were spent covering him up in heated blankets, changing his clothes and bed sheets, because they were constantly soaked from sweat, and running hot baths with Epsom salts to help warm him up and relieve some of his severe muscle and body aches.

I had to help him out of bed and into the tub, but even the slightest touch was painful for him. Once in the tub, I would put hot facecloths over his head, neck, chest, and back, to try to help keep him warm. Hours were spent filling and re-filling the tub with hot water and helping him back and forth between the bed and the bathtub. I felt helpless. All of my efforts to help ease Aaron's pain could not comfort him.

Through all of Aaron's physical pain, he also experienced mental and emotional torture. The withdrawals made him extremely depressed and suicidal. He felt like the pain of the withdrawals was too much to bear. The heartache I experienced watching him suffer through this was almost too much for me to bear.

After days of extreme fatigue, extreme sweats and chills, body aches, anxiety, and depression, Aaron was able to get out of the house and see a doctor. I tried to get him into his regular physician but couldn't get an appointment soon enough, so I took him to a walk-in clinic. The physician at the walk-in made Aaron feel ashamed. She didn't have a good bedside manner to make Aaron feel like he was in a safe place and was cared about. She told us that it was too dangerous for Aaron to quit using opiates cold turkey and provided him a prescription for Dilaudid so he could taper himself off slowly.

I wish I would have known better than to put my trust in this doctor. I honestly think Aaron was through the worst part of the detox and we should have kept fighting to stay off Dilaudid. Another mistake I made was trusting that Aaron could wean himself off the Dilaudid. I ended up having to hide the drugs and only give him what he needed to taper down. I hated this part—I went from being his girlfriend to feeling like his mother.

Aaron tried so hard to convince me he needed more Dilaudid because his leg hurt, and I hated the arguments that ensued when I would tell him no. The arguments would escalate into fights, and there were so many times I felt like giving in because Aaron would almost have me convinced that his leg was in so much pain from the cold weather.

Finally there came a point when Aaron appeared to be doing and feeling well. I believed that we had kicked the addiction and he was drug-free. Knowing what I know now, this was all a lie. Aaron didn't get clean; he had been for a little while, but succumbed to his cravings. I think this was the turning point in

Aaron's addiction, because he started mastering the art of deception. Drug-free Aaron was the furthest from this kind of person, but the addiction had taken over and had altered Aaron's true self. For about seven months, Aaron was able to hide his addiction.

Aaron lost his job shortly after detoxing due to job cutbacks in a hurting economy. He started acting very strange, but I chalked his behaviour up to the fact that he couldn't find a job in his line of work, since there were approximately 10,000 or more people laid off during that time who worked in the oil industry. Aaron was extremely anxious, nervous, depressed, and irritable. He also experienced severe insomnia. All of which I believed was due to the increasing bills Aaron couldn't pay off because he couldn't find a job.

I had asked Aaron if he was doing drugs again, but he somehow convinced me that he wasn't, and made me feel horrible for constantly bringing up the subject. He made me feel terrible for not trusting him, since we both highly believed that trust is one of the most important things in a relationship. He said he would never go back to taking drugs, and would definitely tell me if he had.

Each time I even suggested that I was worried that drugs could be a reason for his odd behaviour, he would get so upset and we would end up in an argument. Somehow, some way, I felt guilty for asking him about taking drugs. However, each time he left the house, even for a minute, I was tearing the house apart and going through his things to look for drugs. I wanted to ensure I had proof before I felt like I could take action with Aaron about using drugs. Every single one of my searches turned up empty.

After months of these ransacks and then putting everything back in its place, I started to believe that Aaron was telling the truth.

However, Aaron's depression, restlessness, and anxiousness escalated to a point that I couldn't deny what my gut was telling me, so I reached out to Aaron's parents for help.

Aaron had tried to commit suicide, so I had taken him to the emergency hospital that had a psychiatric ward. Aaron was 100 percent willing to seek help for his depression, but still adamantly denied being on drugs. As soon as we were triaged through the waiting room, two security guards approached us and told Aaron that he had now been committed to the hospital until the psychiatric doctor could assess him. They took his wallet, phone, shoes, and belt, and threatened me that they would have a warrant out for my arrest if I assisted him in leaving the hospital. Aaron was there willingly and was desperate for help, and they immediately treated us like criminals.

For the next 12 hours, Aaron and I sat in a busy hospital hallway waiting to be seen by a doctor. Finally, just after midnight, Aaron was assessed by the psychiatric doctor. The doctor spent less than 30 minutes with Aaron and determined that he was not "bad enough" to be admitted because he didn't have a "plan" to commit suicide. We were both devastated and frustrated. It was at this time that we felt he would be better off moving to British Columbia with his parents so he could get help from his childhood doctor.

It was only after a series of car accidents in December 2016 and January 2017 that we found out that Aaron was addicted to heroin. Aaron was so ashamed that he tried to take his own life by driving his truck into a telephone pole. Once Aaron confessed, he was so desperate to regain his life and get off opiates. He begged me to go spend a week at his parents' house to help him detox on his own again. I called around to get him into a detox and rehabilitation centre but couldn't find a place that could admit him right away. Through the government-assisted program, I was told that it would take about three months to get him admitted. However, if we paid privately, Aaron could get admitted within 3 to 7 days—but the cost was atrocious! I was quoted anywhere between $7,000 and $14,000 for detox, which would take 1 to 2 weeks, and then approximately $15,000 to $20,000 or more per month in a rehabilitation centre. Aaron just couldn't handle the thought of us paying that much money, even though he desperately wanted to be free of his addiction. I even contacted the show

Intervention Canada, but was told that if Aaron was already detoxing on his own, they couldn't accept him on the show because the whole premise of the show was to document the daily routine of the addict, so he would have to be actively using drugs. I felt like we had no choice but for Aaron to try to detox on his own, since he was so willing to get help immediately. I wanted to take full advantage of how motivated Aaron was to get clean.

The week I spent with Aaron detoxing was very similar to the first time, except Aaron's emotional and mental strength was defeated. He struggled to stay clean that week. I later found out that he was sneaking away from me to get drugs, but soon after was caught by his brother. I believe that it was at this point that Aaron finally got clean. He quickly became his old self again. He found joy in life, had a passion to get his life back on track, and was actively seeking out employment. Aaron was excited to move past his struggles and was looking forward to our life together.

The weekend I spend with Aaron before his death was incredible. He said that he wanted to start showing me how grateful he was that I stayed with him and supported him, and that he was now going to start being the man he knew he could be. I cried happy tears so many times that weekend because I could see the sparkle in Aaron's eyes again and that fiery passion Aaron used to have for life.

Just before Aaron left to return to his parents' house to prepare to go up north for work, we took a picture of us together with the other love of his—his dog, Axl. We cried in each other's arms and didn't want to let go. That was the last time I saw him and felt his embrace. Aaron's last words to me were through a text message he didn't get a chance to send right before he died, which read, "I love you sooo much babes." The police officer took a picture of this unsent message and emailed it to me. I only wish I would have gotten the chance to tell him one last time how much I loved him too. That was April 19, 2017—the day my life changed forever.

Aaron felt so much shame and embarrassment surrounding his addiction. Those drugs stole the most amazing person I have ever met. They robbed Aaron of his whole life—his happiness, his joy, his self-esteem, his self-worth, his pride, his strength, his love of life—and left no one untouched. Everyone who knew Aaron loved him. Those drugs stole a piece of many peoples' hearts. Aaron had so much life to live, and opiates took everything he had.

Drug addictions are so powerful because they isolate people and render not only the addict, but also the addict's friends and family, to feeling helpless and alone. Due to the stigma surrounding drug addictions, far too many people are ashamed to reach out for help. One of my biggest regrets is perpetuating the silence surrounding Aaron's drug addiction. I didn't tell my friends and family about Aaron's struggles. Aaron was afraid of being judged and honestly, so was I. I was afraid people would question why I would stay and support Aaron through his addiction, because I think people could see how the addiction was taking its toll on me. I was afraid of having the extra stress that I thought I would have if people tried to give me their opinions on what was best. It was only after Aaron's death that I started to share our struggle. I was surprised and overwhelmed by the love and support I received from my closest friends and family. No one judged Aaron, and no one questioned why I stayed. Everyone just wanted me to know how much they loved Aaron and how much they wished they could have been a part of Aaron's fight.

After Aaron's death, I struggled with feelings of guilt—I should have done more. I should have recognized the signs earlier. I should have done things differently. To help me learn to live with my guilt and my grief, I went to a grief counsellor. It was through these sessions that I realized that there will always be things we wish we could have done differently, but the reality is, we did the best we could. I did the best that I could, and never did anything to intentionally harm Aaron; in fact, everything I did was to help him. I tried the tough love approach and the unconditional love approach. I tried providing him with resources and being his support system. I did everything out of love.

I have been working hard on forgiving myself and taking the time to work through my grief. Everyone says that "time heals all wounds," but no one tells you that you will not heal 100 percent, and that it may take years before you even start to feel the slightest bit of healing.

I have been told time and time again that I just need to get back into my old routine, but what they don't realize is that my old routine is gone because Aaron was a part of it. I have to forge a new routine, and this takes a lot of time, a lot of self-love, and a lot of heartache. I am forever changed by these events, both for the good and bad. Aaron taught me what true love was. He taught me to enjoy every minute and be present in the moment. Aaron helped me see that I am worthy of love and that I need to be kind to myself. I have never met anyone like Aaron, and I know I never will again.

Every relationship is unique, and therefore everyone's grief is unique. There is no time frame or step-by-step path to take in our journey to healing. There isn't a day that goes by that I don't think of Aaron, but I am so thankful that he chose me to spend his last years with. He was truly a gift.

I learned that it is our silence that keeps the stigma alive. Don't fight alone—it only gives these drugs more power.

STEROIDS

Anabolic Steroids - Aaron was hooked on these for a while when he was doing his bodybuilding, and I will highlight the symptoms we all noticed.

Anabolic steroids are synthetic variations of the male sex hormone testosterone. The proper term for these compounds is *anabolic-androgenic steroids*. "Anabolic" refers to muscle building, and "androgenic" refers to increased male sex characteristics. Some common names for anabolic steroids are gear, juice, roids, and stackers.

(www.drugabuse.gov/publications/drugfacts/anabolic-steroids)

Some athletes and others who abuse steroids believe they can avoid unwanted side effects or maximize the drugs' effects by taking them in ways that include:

Cycling - taking doses for a period of time, stopping for a time, and then restarting.

Stacking - combining two or more different types of steroids.

Pyramiding - slowly increasing the dose or frequency of abuse, reaching a peak amount, and then gradually tapering off.

There is no scientific evidence that any of these practices reduce the harmful medical consequences of these drugs.

How do anabolic steroids affect the brain?

Anabolic steroids work differently from other drugs of abuse; they do not have the same short-term effects on the brain. The most important difference is that steroids do not trigger rapid increases in the brain chemical dopamine, which causes the "high" that drives people to abuse other substances. However, long-term steroid abuse can act on some of the same brain pathways and chemicals—including dopamine, serotonin, and opioid systems—that are affected by other drugs. This may result in a significant effect on mood and behaviour.

Short-Term Effects

Abuse of anabolic steroids may lead to mental problems, such as:

Paranoid (extreme, unreasonable) jealousy

Extreme irritability

Delusions—false beliefs of ideas

Impaired judgment

Extreme mood swings can also occur, including "roid rage"— angry feelings and behaviour that may lead to violence.

Aside from mental problems, steroid use commonly causes severe acne. It also causes the body to swell, especially in the hands and feet.

Long-Term Effects

Anabolic steroid abuse may lead to serious, even permanent, health problems, such as:

Kidney problems or failure

Liver damage

Enlarged heart, high blood pressure, and changes in blood cholesterol, all of which increase the risk of stroke and heart attack, even in young people.

Aaron was having problems with his heart skipping beats, and a few times he passed out at the gym. Three or four times he had to go to emergency and have his heart re-started because the beats to his heart were not normal. That was a huge warning sign to us. We had several talks with him, telling him that we know it is the steroids doing this. Of course his answer was no, it wasn't the steroids. (At that time we had no idea that he also had a problem with drugs.)

Several other effects are gender- and age-specific:

In men:

Shrinking testicles

Decreased sperm count

Baldness

Development of breasts

Increased risk for prostate cancer

In women:

Growth of facial hair or excess body hair

Male-pattern baldness

Changes in or stop in the menstrual cycle

Enlarged clitoris

Deepened voice

In teens:

Stunted growth (when high hormone levels from steroids signal to the body to stop bone growth too early)

Stunted height (if teens use steroids before their growth spurt)

Even though anabolic steroids do not cause the same high as other drugs, they can lead to addiction. People may continue to abuse steroids despite physical problems, high costs to buy the drugs, and negative effects on their relationships. These behaviours reflect steroids' addictive potential. Research has further found that some steroid users turn to other drugs, such as opioids, to reduce sleep problems and irritability caused by steroids.

People who abuse steroids may experience withdrawal symptoms when they stop use, including:

Mood swings

Fatigue

Restlessness

Loss of appetite

Sleep problems

Decreased sex drive (I only know about this because he told his dad.)

Steroid cravings

One of the more serious withdrawal symptoms is depression, which can sometimes lead to suicide attempts.

COCAINE

Cocaine is a powerfully addictive stimulant drug made from the leaves of the coca plant native to South America. Although health care providers can use it for valid medical purposes, such as local anesthesia for some surgeries, cocaine is an illegal drug. As a street drug, cocaine looks like a fine, white, crystal power. Street dealers often mix it with things like cornstarch, talcum powder, or flour, to increase profits. They may also mix it with other drugs, such as the stimulant amphetamine. *(www.drugabuse.gov/publications/drugfacts-cocaine)*

Popular nicknames are blow, coke, crack, and rock.

Cocaine increases levels of the natural chemical messenger dopamine in brain circuits controlling pleasure and movement.

How does cocaine affect the brain?

Cocaine increases levels of the natural chemical messenger dopamine in brain circuits controlling pleasure and movement.

Normally, the brain releases dopamine in these circuits in response to potential rewards, like the smell of good food. It then recycles back into the cell that released it, shutting off the signal between nerve cells. Cocaine prevents dopamine from recycling, causing excessive amounts to build up between nerve cells. This floor of dopamine ultimately disrupts normal brain communication and causes cocaine's high.

Short-term effects of cocaine include:

Extreme happiness and energy
Mental alertness
Hypersensitivity to sight, sound, and touch
Irritability
Paranoia—extreme and unreasonable distrust of others.

Some people find that cocaine helps them perform simple physical and mental tasks more quickly, although others experience the opposite effect. Large amounts of cocaine can lead to bizarre, unpredictable, and violent behaviour.

Cocaine's effects appear almost immediately, and disappear within a few minutes to an hour. How long the effects last and how intense they are depend on the method of use. Injecting or smoking cocaine produces a quicker and stronger but shorter-lasting high than snorting. The high from snorting cocaine may last 15 to 30 minutes. The high from smoking may last 5 to 10 minutes.

<u>Other health effects of cocaine use include</u>:

Constricted blood vessels

Dilated pupils

Nausea

Raised body temperature and blood pressure

Faster heartbeat

Tremors and muscle twitches

Restlessness

Long-term effects

Snorting: loss of sense of smell, nosebleeds, frequent runny nose, and problems with swallowing

Consuming by mouth: severe bowel decay from reduced blood flow

Needle injection: high risk for contracting HIV, hepatitis C, and other blood-borne diseases. However, even people involved with non-needle cocaine use place themselves at a risk for HIV because cocaine impairs judgment, which can lead to risky sexual behaviour with infected partners.

Can a person overdose on cocaine?

Yes, an overdose occurs when the person uses too much of a drug and has a toxic reaction that results in serious, harmful symptoms or death.

Death from overdose can occur on the first use of cocaine or unexpectedly thereafter. Many people who use cocaine also drink alcohol at the same time, which is particularly risky and can lead to overdose. Others mix cocaine with heroin, another dangerous—and deadly—combination.

Some of the most frequent and severe health consequences leading to overdose involve the heart and blood vessels, including irregular heart rhythm and heart attacks, and the nerves, including seizures and strokes.

As with other drugs, repeated use of cocaine can cause long-term changes in the brain's reward circuit and other brain systems, which may lead to addiction. The reward circuit eventually adapts to the excess dopamine brought on by the drug. As a result, people take stronger and more frequent doses to achieve the same high and feel relief from initial withdrawal.

Withdrawal symptoms include:
Depression
Fatigue
Increased appetite
Unpleasant dreams and insomnia
Slowed thinking

Short-term effects include:

Constricted blood vessels

Nausea

Faster heartbeat

Extreme happiness and energy

Irritability

Paranoia

Long-term effects

Nosebleeds

Severe bowel decay

Higher risk of contracting HIV, hepatitis C, and other blood-borne diseases

Malnourishment

Restlessness

Severe paranoia with auditory hallucinations

A person can overdose on cocaine, which can lead to death. Behavioural therapy may be used to treat cocaine addiction.

While no government-approved medicines are currently available to treat cocaine addiction, researchers are testing some treatments.

HEROIN

Heroin is an opioid drug made from morphine, a natural substance taken from the seed pod of the various opium poppy plants grown in Southeast and Southwest Asia, Mexico, and Colombia. Heroin can be a white or brown powder, or a black, sticky substance known as black tar heroin. Other common names for heroin include big H, horse, hell dust, and smack. *(www.drugabuse.gov/publications/drugfacts-heroin)*

Heroin enters the brain rapidly and binds the opioid receptors on cells located in many areas, especially those involved in feelings of pain and pleasure and in controlling heart rate, sleeping, and breathing.

Prescription opioid pain medicines such as OxyContin and Vicodin have effects similar to heroin. Research suggests that misuse of these drugs may open the door to heroin use. Nearly 80 percent of Americans using heroin (including those in treatment) reported misusing prescription opioids first.

Short-term effects

Dry mouth

Warm flushing of the skin

Heavy feeling in the arms and legs

Nausea and vomiting

Severe itching

Clouded mental functioning

Going "on the nod," a back-and-forth state of being conscious and semiconscious

Long-term effects

Insomnia

Collapsed veins for people who inject the drug

Damaged tissue inside the nose for people who sniff or snort it

Infection of the heart lining and valves

Abscesses (swollen tissue filled with pus)

Constipation and stomach cramping

Liver and kidney disease

Lung complications, including pneumonia

Mental disorders, such as depression and antisocial personality disorder

Sexual dysfunction for men

Irregular menstrual cycles for women

Other potential effects

Heroin often contains additives, such as sugar, starch, or powdered milk, which can clog blood vessels leading to the lungs, liver, kidneys, or brain, causing permanent damage. Also, sharing drug injection equipment and having impaired judgment from drug use can increase the risk of contracting infectious diseases such as HIV and hepatitis.

Can a person overdose on heroin?

Yes, a heroin overdose occurs when a person uses enough of the drug to produce a life-threatening reaction or death. Heroin overdoses have increased in recent years. Naloxone is a medicine that can treat a heroin overdose when given right away, though more than one dose may be needed.

When people overdose on heroin, their breathing often slows or stops. This can decrease the amount of oxygen that reaches the brain, a condition called hypoxia. Hypoxia can have short- and long-term mental effects and effects on the nervous system, including coma and permanent brain damage.

Is heroin addictive?

Heroin is highly addictive. People who regularly use heroin often develop a tolerance, which means that they need higher and/or more frequent doses of the drug to get the desired effects. A substance use disorder (SUD) is when continued use of the drug causes issues, such as health problems and failure to meet responsibilities at work, school, or home. An SUD can range from mild to severe, the most severe form being addiction.

Those who are addicted to heroin and stop using the drug abruptly may have severe withdrawal. Withdrawal symptoms—which can begin as early as a few hours after the drug was last taken—include:

Restlessness
Severe muscle and bone pain (this one was hard to tell because of his accident)
Sleep problems
Diarrhea and vomiting
Cold flashes with goose bumps ("cold turkey")
Uncontrollable leg movements ("kicking the habit") (fidgeting badly)
Severe heroin cravings (Probably)

Researchers are studying long-term opioid addiction effects on the brain. Studies have shown some loss of the brain's white matter associated with heroin use, which may affect decision-making, behaviour, control, and responses to stressful situations. *(www.drugabuse.gov/publications/drugfacts-heroin)*

A range of treatments including medicines and behavioural therapies are effective in helping people stop heroin use. However, treatment plans should be individualized to meet the needs of the patient.

A person can overdose on heroin. Naloxone is a medicine that can treat a heroin overdose when given right away, though more than one dose may be needed.

Heroin can lead to addiction, a form of substance use disorder. Withdrawal symptoms include severe muscle and bone pain, sleep problems, diarrhea and vomiting, and severe heroin cravings.

FENTANYL, THE KILLER

Fentanyl is a powerful synthetic opioid analgesic that is similar to morphine but is 50 to 100 times more potent. It is a schedule II prescription drug, (A controlled substance - a high potential for abuse which may lead to severe psychological or physical dependence. www.deadiversion.usdoj.gov/schedules) and it is typically used to treat patients with severe pain or to manage pain after surgery. It is also sometimes used to treat patients with chronic pain who are physically tolerant to other opioids. In its prescription form, fentanyl is known by such names as Actiq, Duragesic, and Sublimaze. Street names for fentanyl or for fentanyl-laced heroin include Apache, China Girl, China White, Dance Fever, Friend, Goodfella, Jackpot, Murder 8, TNT, and Tango and Cash.

How do people use fentanyl?

When prescribed by a physician, fentanyl is often administered via injection, transdermal patch, or in lozenges. However, the fentanyl and fentanyl analogues associated with recent overdoses are produced in clandestine laboratories. This non-pharmaceutical fentanyl is sold in the following forms: as a powder; spiked on blotter paper; mixed with or substituted for heroin; or as tablets that mimic other, less potent opioids. People can swallow, snort, or inject fentanyl, or they can put blotter paper in their mouths so that fentanyl is absorbed through the mucous membrane.

How does fentanyl affect the brain?

Like heroin, morphine, and other opioid drugs, fentanyl works by binding to the body's opioid receptors, which are found in areas of the brain that control pain and emotions. When opioid drugs bind to these receptors, they can drive up dopamine levels in the brain's reward areas, producing a state of euphoria and relaxation. Fentanyl's effects resemble those of heroin and include euphoria, drowsiness, nausea, confusion, constipation, sedation, tolerance, addiction, respiratory depression and arrest, unconsciousness, coma, and death.

Why is fentanyl dangerous?

Opioid receptors are also found in the areas of the brain that control breathing rate. High doses of opioids, especially potent opioids such as fentanyl, can cause breathing to stop completely, which can lead to death. The high potency of fentanyl greatly increases risk of overdose, especially if a person who uses drugs is unaware that a powder or pill contains fentanyl. Fentanyl sold on the street can be mixed with heroin or cocaine, which markedly amplifies its potency and potential dangers.

The medication naloxone is an opioid receptor antagonist that reverses opioid overdose and restores normal respiration. Overdoses of fentanyl should be treated immediately with naloxone, and may require higher doses to successfully reverse the overdose.

Short-term effects

Reduced feelings of pain

Euphoria

Relaxation

Those seeking the effects above will often abuse fentanyl by taking it without a prescription, using high doses, or mixing it with other drugs. **All of these situations can turn fatal**.

If fentanyl abuse and addiction has a hold on you, a friend, or someone you love, call **1-877-768-9614.**

Side effects

Nausea

Vomiting

Constipation

Altered heart rate

Slowed breathing rate

Confusion

Hallucinations

Weakness

Sweating

Itchy skin

Constricted pupils

Seizures

Long-term effects

Showing signs of poor judgment in both work and personal situations

Increase your risk for anoxic injury (damage due to significantly decreased oxygen in the body tissues) and multiple organ system damage

Significantly increase your risk of overdose and death

Do harm to your personal life and relationships

Initiate or worsen pre-existing mental health conditions, including depression and/or labile (frequently changing) moods

Fentanyl overdose symptoms

Difficulty swallowing

Extreme fatigue

Dizziness and fainting

Shallow, difficult breathing/respiratory arrest

Cardiac arrest

Non-responsiveness to painful stimuli

Severe confusion

Obtundation (altered level of consciousness)

Detox and withdrawal

oss of appetite

Tremors

Agitation

Anxiety/panic

Fever and chills

Sweating

Nausea/vomiting

Runny nose

Diarrhea

Intense drug cravings.

AARON'S PLAN ON HELPING OTHERS

While my husband and I were in Mexico on vacation in 2017, Aaron had a desire to help others get off of fentanyl. He knew how bad it was because he had lost four of his friends since January of that year up until he passed away in April. They had all passed away from fentanyl. He was so deeply depressed by this that he wrote down his thoughts and plans of how he was going to help. This is another reason why I know Aaron would not have taken fentanyl willingly. Why would he want to chance dying and then not be able to go through with this plan? Again, these are all pages in Aaron's handwriting. He wanted to call his program **LIFESAVERS.** He had even started a GoFundMe page for this project, but it didn't have a chance to get off the ground.

LIFESAVERS

1st facse Funding

Objective: To promote safe & aware partying, due to increase in fen. overdoses

Locations: Clubs, bars, community parading, social network, app, website.

Mannor: Will not enforce, must merely offer info, safety, naloxone to anyone interested @ door establishments.

Plan: To show up @ clubs & inform those entering/leaving. Patrol communities looking for activity, contact party holders.

- Introduce
- Inform
- Present
- Leave.

Places to look for funding: Club owners, bar owners, (community) donations, THE CITY, Hospitals.

Means of Communication: Social media = Facebook
- App
- Website

Lifesaverz@html.com
About s

Facebook

- make page for ppl to interact
- make posts from ppl private to public.
Only admin can see.

(Public Page, private posts, member to member etc.

↳ App & page will have a memorial to fent loss
- Also counter of lives saved

App → "FAITHBOOK" Will direct Admin/Employee where parties are in their
comm. over a map so they can attend & present

- IILP

Must be for admin & Employee only. Police cannot
have access to ensure personal privacy
Update Members can post to admins where their
friends or so & so can be found to drop this off.

Website: - Videos on demos
              of administering
- effects of drug
- where to be found
- signs of use & OD
- Help Link to AA
        & Detox

Advertising: • Social Media
- FB   - NEWS
- App
- Website

- Phone Book
- Internet
- Google
- Vehicle Signage
- local newspapers
- Banners outside of & at downtown.

.

How To Lift Off: A: Start small, on my own
door to door & patrol.
B: Contact city, Set up for meeet,
present idea. Contact Hosp, Clinics,
clubs, bars,

C: Investors

- Will Need Large Shop
- Storage for med spp.
- Vehicles
- Staff

- $

FOCUS - Get more Naloxone kits to house parties
Homes, private settings, areas medics are NOT
    - To find Designated/Sober person in household
        to main demo infront of
            - All others may watch

* Offer Very Discounted Price at Kit if
Contacting outside of a patrol.

Phone Number

250 --- SAVE (8172)
780 --- SAVE
My Many --- SAVE

Expansion

- Provincial (small city outs - Vernon
                            - Kelowna
                            - Vancouver
- Federal
        - Spread to Alberta ✓ Same approach
        - Across to East Coast
- International

Supplies: All standard First Aid Kit = _____ COST

· Heart Monitor / BP machine : _____

· Naloxone Kits - Come w/ : _____
instruction

Employee - Mandatory First AID/CPR Training.

Vehicle - Will be marked w/ some sort of
flashing lights or solid color to inform ppl
when vehicle is in areas.

Operation Costs
· Website/App cost.

• Fuel
- Wear & tear
- Naloxone kit
- First Aid kit

136

- Start @ Methadone Clinic to acquire kits.
  - Prevent Ambulance driveaway costs if possible

- Take close impact on Hospitals medical clinics
- Need to be funded gov't,
  - Will take down on annual costs to medical System
  - medics won't be overwhelmed by OD cases can focus on other areas of jobs.
  -

- Find out Annual Expenses Prov./Fed, or OD cases & overall
  - Lives lost pro/fed.
  - Savings to System
  -

Detox Centers - Get Sponsors
                - promoting
                - page links

Interior Health
           - Harm Reduction
           - Overdose Protection   NO MOBILE
                                        UNITS I CAN SEE

Primary Care - Karl : Wednesday
                        (250.

I don't understand what is happening in our world today. We all had plans for our children. To see them grow into beautiful adults and have their own families. We nurtured our children with so much love because that's who we are as parents. Staying up late at night worrying because they hadn't arrived home yet. Not being able to close your eyes until you knew they were safe at home. Trying to educate them with safety in mind, teaching them right from wrong. Taking them to karate, baseball, sports competitions, bowling, snowboarding, boating, camping, swimming lessons, piano lessons, etc. Making sure they were kept busy and off the streets.

Even when they leave home we are still worrying about their health and welfare. Helping them with money even though you say enough! We did all that we were supposed to do. Yet it wasn't enough—when is it enough? I wish so badly I could turn back the clock to April 2017. I had no idea that my son hid so much from us. At what moment in our kids' lives did things change? Why did it have to go this far? Did we as parents do something to deserve this? It is so hard to keep faith when you see how many of us are going through the same thing. What a miserable world we live in. We need CHANGE! We need HELP from the government before we lose a whole generation!

———————

ANONYMOUS

Now that I am in Heaven, I know that life for you there just isn't the same. I want you to know that I hear you say how much you miss me and love me every day. Yes, I still hear you. I love you so much too. My love for you will never waver from Heaven. I can't say that I miss you because, you see, missing you is a negative emotion, and we simply don't have negative emotions in Heaven. And so, instead of missing you for all of the years that you have left in your life, I will love you through them.

I know it is hard to continue on when you feel you are walking through life without me, but I want you to know that I am right here next to you. I walk through your life with you now, guiding you and helping you along the way. Our relationship never ended when I graduated to Heaven, it is simply different now. Heaven is all around you. Heaven is truly only three feet off of your floor. I want you to look for the signs that I leave for you from Heaven. You won't have to look very hard because I will surround you with signs in so many different ways. You see, I am limitless when it comes to leaving you signs. Birds, butterflies, silly shaped rocks, rainbows, clouds that look like me, electronic mishaps, songs on your radio, coins, feathers . . . oh, I wouldn't begin to be able to tell you how many different kinds of signs I can bring into your path. When you see the signs I send, don't let your conscious mind tell you that it wasn't from me, because it really was.

Sometimes you may miss the signs I send you because it is hard to see the beauty in the world around you through tears, and that is okay. I will just keep sending signs of love until those tears clear. I am not missing out on your milestones or the milestones within our family. I love the way you think of me so often. I think the ways that you and the family have honored me since I journeyed home to Heaven are pretty amazing.

Please try not to dwell on the day and way that I passed each day, for my legacy of love that I left behind for you is so much more beautiful than my passing. It hurts you to think of my passing, and that hurt is not the best part of me that I left for you. I want you to hold onto our sweet memories that we share with one another.

When you find yourself in a day of tears, please just replace one of those tears with your favorite memory of me. I will sit with you as you remember me and enjoy the memory with you. I know you would love to see me in dreams every night as you go to sleep. I would love to be there in your dreams each night as well. When you say out loud, "I never see you in my dreams," it places blocks in my way because your energy says that you don't see me. I want to help you with that. I want you to change that phrase to, "I look forward to seeing you in my dreams in your perfect timing." It will help you to place this positive focus on seeing me in your dreams when the timing is right.

The reason I don't come every night in your dreams is because you really do need space to work through your grief as well. You see, you are gaining more strength through your grief than you ever knew you could carry in life. Part of that strength is my gift to you, and that gift will only make sense someday when you return home to Heaven here with me. We spend our lives there living for our spiritual growth. Some of the most beautiful and strong spirits write some of the most difficult paths, and I want you to be so proud of yourself for the life you are living with all of the obstacles you placed within your path.

I also want you to know how extremely proud of you I am as I watch you learn and grow from Heaven. God didn't punish you when I went to Heaven before you. I simply reached my soul's beautiful goal of growth in life. I reached that amazing goal before you, and it didn't mean that I left you for one moment. I graduated to the next part of my eternal journey in Heaven. Oh, you should have seen it when I got here!! All of our family and friends who graduated to Heaven before me were right at my side to greet me when I arrived! Even pets that we had along the way were waiting with smiles and wags as I walked into Heaven's light!

I went into a review of my life after I arrived, and it was truly amazing to see all of the lives I touched with mine. I got to re-live my life through the eyes of each and every person that my life touched along the way. It was beautiful to watch my life through your eyes as well. Don't worry, when you get here, you will get to review your life through everyone's eyes, as well as your own, and even through mine. There will be moments you are extremely proud of, and there will also be moments that you will recognize that you could have handled differently. But the beauty of those moments is that you are living and in your life, not everything will be perfect, and that is just part of our growth. None of us can take back the things we could have done differently, but we sure can grow from those moments.

Of course, me telling you this now gives you an opportunity to look at the days in your future differently so that you will be proud of them when you look back.

I didn't have to make myself a home when I arrived to Heaven because I already had one. You see, I lived in Heaven before I lived there on Earth with you, and I simply returned to my beautiful home in Heaven. You will remember it too when you get here.

The colors here in Heaven aren't like anything you have there on Earth! The light that fills the air lifts our souls with love, for it is made of God. The Angel's Choir has such a Heavenly sound that it brings peaceful showers of love down upon you all on Earth. The weather here is perfect, always. Time doesn't exist here, which is really nice, too; I mean, we don't have to run around Heaven looking at our watches on our spirit wrists, worried about being late for anything, ha ha. You see, you can't place a time on Eternity.

We don't work here in Heaven the way you all work there on Earth, but we do work. We work on our spiritual growth, as we are part of God and we are always working on the beautiful evolution of our soul's growth and strength. Just remember as you walk through your life each and every day that I am right there at your side. I cheer you on in your times of greatness and I wipe your tears in your moments of pain. So what if you have a day of tears; I will stay at your side for comfort.

I can tell you that I am most proud of you as you get out and live life to its fullest. I don't want you to think that you can no longer live because I am "gone," because I am not gone at all. Carry me with you in all that you do, for I am here. The dreams that you wish you could have lived out with me in life are still possible—and don't worry, I won't miss them.

My biggest message of all in this letter from Heaven to you is that I am perfect; don't worry about me. I love you, and I am with you for always. I want to see you live life to its fullest. I want to see you catch your dreams, and I see you and hear you always, both when you speak out loud and even when you speak silently to me in your mind.

Someday this will all make perfect sense when you get to Heaven with me, so don't worry that it doesn't make sense now. Just know that you are a miracle because you are made of God, and because you are a miracle, you are capable of creating miracles as well. I LOVE YOU . . .

DAY ONE CONTINUED

While we waited for the paramedics to clean up Aaron, the police constable wanted to interview each one of us separately in a private room. The last thing I wanted to do was talk to someone about Aaron and his medical issues and be questioned for a half-hour. That was so difficult—but I had to carry on, because I wanted the prick caught that poisoned my son. (I say poisoned my son because the police had uncovered several foil packets in Aaron's room, assuming it was heroin or something of that nature, but they were also worried that there was fentanyl amongst it.)

So through a lot of tears I answered all that I could, then he brought in Jim and Daniel. I spent all the time I could in Aaron's room with Aaron until the coroner arrived to pick Aaron up. My mind was numb. I didn't know what to do about anything. Our son was gone forever—that's FOREVER! It was like the last 30 years never existed because he wasn't here anymore. My brain was telling me to do all kinds of things that I would never, ever, even contemplate before. I wanted to be with him, hold his hand while he made his journey to Heaven. I didn't care about myself anymore, or what would happen to me. All I wanted was to be with Aaron.

But I guess my subconscious kept interfering with my thoughts, trying to keep me from doing the unthinkable. I still had two other sons and a husband, and I couldn't imagine putting them through another horrific experience. It took months for me to stop finding a way to be with Aaron. I kept telling myself that I wasn't afraid to die. (I still am not afraid.) But my thinking then was to find a way to do it without hurting my family. I thought of an easy way out because if I did something that left me brain dead or a paraplegic, that would mean my family would have to take care of me for the rest of my life and I couldn't put them through that, because then I would have no control over finishing the job. So I took seven of my Tylenol 3s at once, hoping that would make me overdose. (This was the day after Aaron had passed). Nothing happened except I was tired. I guessed that since I had been on this med for so many years for my chronic back pain that I was now immune to them. So just before bed, I took another four. If my subconscious didn't keep kicking in, I would have taken the whole bottle.

We are now at seven months since Aaron passed away. When my husband and sister told me to start a diary, I really wasn't interested. The last thing I wanted to do was start writing my feelings down, because I didn't care. It was some time after that that I decided to go ahead with it, but I didn't write down every day's feelings because they were pretty much the same. What I did do was write down the important ones.

Before the coroner's office arrived at the house, Daniel took off the tie that was wrapped around Aaron's forehead, and we were shaken by what we saw. He had a gash about two inches in length, and so deep you could see inside. With the help from the officer and others, we came to the conclusion that he smoked something in his bathroom and passed out. He hit the toilet lid that was sitting in the upright position (that's where the blood was). The curved section of the lid pushed through his forehead. He must have been in horrific pain but he was too proud to walk 75 feet down the hall to our bedroom to tell us what happened. We also did not hear any noise. Our dogs didn't even bark.

What Aaron did do was this: he cleaned the whole bathroom of as much blood as he could find. We found the toilet brush and two cleaners in the bathroom. He obviously did not want us to find the mess. Then he went to his room and texted his ex-girlfriend's sister, Cori, in Edmonton, Alberta, who is a nurse, and asked her what to do, along with a picture of his forehead. Sometime either before his text or after, he took a sleeping pill. Maybe for the pain; and thought he would feel better in the morning if he had a good night's sleep? I don't know.

After looking at his phone, we had seen that it was around 1:30 a.m. our time, which would have been 2:30 a.m. Cori's time, and she would have been sleeping. So once again he did not get a reply, yet also did not want to come tell us what happened.

The last text on his phone was to his girlfriend, Shauna. It said: " I love you sooo much babes" and then he must have dropped his phone because he didn't even have the strength to send it.

We had let Shauna know at a later time about the text, but we didn't send it to her until she was ready for it. Both Jim and Daniel called Shauna in Edmonton to tell her about Aaron. The poor girl; to get this phone call at work was so devastating. She had to get people to take her home, and we spoke every day on the phone until she and her mother came to stay with us for a week during the funeral.

We still cannot believe he is gone. It just seems so unfathomable, like a nightmare you can't wake up from. Yet everyone else seems to go about their daily routine like nothing has changed. You get times when you get mad at people because you see them laughing, eating, watching TV, shopping, and having fun. You want to yell out to them: "Do You Not Care That My Son Died!" Yet they don't know you or your son.

It's the most difficult thing any parent could ever go through. We couldn't watch TV for a long time. I felt guilty if I sat down and watched TV or listened to music or did anything that Aaron would have done. Why? In my mind I felt if Aaron can no longer do it, then I won't either, because it wasn't fair.

I spent as much time with Aaron as I could before he was taken away. I just held him and kissed him and talked to him. During that time, Jim would come in, Daniel would come in, and they would talk or just stand there looking at him. Our friends Al and Darlene also came in to say goodbye to him (which was difficult, because they loved him and it brought back memories of their son, who passed away 18 years ago).

I walked out of Aaron's room for a while to get some fresh air. While I was outside, I noticed the coroner had arrived, but I assumed someone would come get me and tell me I could say goodbye one more time if I wanted to. But no one did—they loaded him and left. I came running back into the house to see that he was no longer in his bedroom. I cried like crazy again. I said, "I wanted to say goodbye again." I just didn't want to see my baby leave my side! I didn't know how he would be treated without me at his side. Even though his soul was now in Heaven, his body was still here on earth, my blood. I didn't want anyone abusing his body or just treating him like another drug addict. He was so much more than that. He was our life, our blood, our soul, our son!

Now the phone started to ring and it didn't stop. I didn't want to see anyone or talk to anyone. I just wanted to be left alone. Jim's family was to come up to the Okanagan to stay with us for a few days. I love them dearly, and I know they wanted to be with us, but I even told my own family that wanted to come up and be with us no. "I'll let you know when the service is and you can come then." I just didn't want anyone around except Jim and Daniel.

Jim's family did come up and they were a great help, but it was so hard to try to stay strong in front of them—or in front of anyone, for that matter.

Aaron's cell phone was still getting texts, and we noticed one in particular that would text Aaron asking if that "did it for him," and more texts after that. We found out that this person was the one that sold Aaron his fatal dose of whatever he took. We gave the phone to the police, so now they know who and where this person lives. But up until this day, still nothing has been done. We have called the RCMP several times, to no avail. So I had enough. I wrote a letter to Mike Farnworth MLA; he is the minister of Public Safety.

This letter was written October 13, 2017.

Honourable Mike Farnworth;

I am writing to you in hopes of finding justice for my son Aaron James M.

This is my son Aaron, He was a normal child in a normal upbringing with a heart of gold. He got into a horrible snowboarding accident in Jasper AB January of 2014, after having 4 surgeries he became addicted to prescription drugs. The doctor in Alberta kept prescribing him the strongest drugs you could get. After a while the doctor's cut him off with no counselling or suggestions for counselling. Well suffice it to say, Aaron was hooked.... not surprised! Again, no help getting weaned off of these narcotics just an abrupt door slammed in his face. Aaron tried to help himself by getting into Bodybuilding to strengthen his body back up and he wanted to go into competition so he worked very hard at trying to help himself but the pain in his leg was too much. Well he talked to a buddy of his regarding his pain and of course his buddy steered him in the direction of no return. Heroine. The worst drug anyone could ever inflict upon themselves. My beautiful naive son, not knowing what he was getting himself into took advice from someone he only knew a short time, instead of coming to us, (his parents). The day he started this was the beginning of the end.

This went on for sometime 2-3 years without us even knowing. Sept of 2016 his girlfriend called us crying telling us what he was on and that he made her promise not to tell us because he was so ashamed of himself and was afraid we would disown him as a son. We were stunned at the news, (Aaron our son doing one of the worst drugs on this planet.... that can't be true). Aaron was an honour roll student, he wanted to try to better himself every chance he got. He had a great job servicing oil pumps on rigs and overseas as well. He was an excellent piano player, drummer, wake boarder, snowboarder and loved fishing. He had so many talents and could do anything he put his mind to. He had a heart of gold he would help a stranger without even thinking of any consequences. After his injury he was on disability for several months.... he was wheelchair bound for a couple of months. When he did go back to work on light duties for a few months..... they laid him off. That was a huge hit to him and I know things spiralled downwards after that.

In September we flew him back home to BC and took care of him, brought him to the doctor, tried to get him into a Detox center in Vernon to no avail.... They said he wasn't bad enough... We could not believe what we were hearing. He was to go to see our family doctor everyday or at least call. We took care of him through his Detox which was just horrible. He was our son.... I loved him with all my heart, I would do anything to keep my son alive.... I would give my own life for him.

On April 18 around 7:30pm he was in Vernon and had made a phone call to someone to meet with him.... (after being clean for approx 6-8 weeks) he slipped......and bought we are assuming heroin. But that's not what the toxicology report said. It was 100% pure Fentanyl. My son died through the early hours of the morning. He exasperated .... the morning of April 19 my youngest son's birthday I went into Aarons room to wake him up because we were expecting a Real Estate Agent to show up and Aaron was sleeping in too long. Suffice it to say..... you can only imagine my horror of finding my son's cold dead body in his bed. I wanted to die right then and there. I blamed God for taking him from us.

Aaron was 30. Nov 19 will be 7 months that Aaron has been gone from us. I am having as difficult time now with his death as I did the day he passed.

We have the name, phone number etc. of the person that sold him this killing drug and all the police keep saying is the wheels of justice turn very slow. WHY CAN'T WE ARREST THAT PERSON !!! We know who it was. That same guy even texted Aarons phone a few times after Aaron passed away. The police have all the information yet nothing is being done. I am so mad. I hear on the news that Alberta and Ontario are charging the dealers with manslaughter. Well my son Aaron James Mennear was MURDERED and we want JUSTICE! please help us. I cannot go on living like this knowing this person has gotten away with it.

Lumby Police Detachment

I remain,

After three weeks I had heard nothing back, so I emailed again. Then about a week later I got a call from a female. She expressed how sorry she was about what had happened to Aaron, but I did not get the help I wanted. She told me to call the chief superintendent of the Kelowna detachment, since he was the big boss, and I wasn't getting anywhere with our detachments in Lumby or Vernon. So now we have left several messages with them. One constable called and left a message saying that he and the chief superintendent would be on holidays for a week and would call back. Never did. Why am I surprised? So the back-and-forth calling continues.

Jim and I had never had to make funeral arrangements before. We had helped family members with theirs, but never had to do it on our own before. So we were really lost—not to mention devastated—that we have to have a funeral for one of our boys. When we finally picked a funeral home, we were told that they wouldn't receive the body until the coroner had finished with the toxicology report, which actually took a week . We were quite upset that it took that long because we had family from out of town, and even out of province, that were coming.

Finally, late in the day on Monday April 24, the coroner's office called us to say that they released Aaron's body to the funeral home. So on the Tuesday we called the local newspaper to have his obituary put in so we could get on with the service. The only day available was that Friday, which didn't help us much, because the ad didn't get into the paper until that Friday morning. So we called everyone we could think of to let them know when the service was going to be. We had expected several hundred people because of all the friends Aaron had. But with not being able to call everyone, and the late notice in the paper, just under 100 people showed up.

At the service, I kept thinking, *This should be Aaron's wedding we are attending, not his funeral.* The last thing I would have ever dreamed of happening, was happening. We were saying goodbye to our beautiful boy.

Our Lives Will Never Be The Same From This Day Forward

———————————

2017 DIARY

Early Fall, one morning before getting out of bed my husband Jim said to me I have this terrible feeling inside and its telling me that we are going to be going through a shit storm.

Oct 23 2016	-	Shadow, my precious dog, passed away four days before his 16th birthday. His death was the start of the train wreck.
April 19 2017	-	Aaron passed away
April 28 2017	-	Aaron's service
May 2 2017	-	Our dog Princessa has her eye removed because of glaucoma
May 13 2017	-	My niece's dog Jake passed away
May 24 2017	-	Emily (Aaron's cousin of 33 years) passed away
June 11 2017	-	Emily's service
June 21 2017	-	My mother passed away
June 27 2017	-	My mother's service

| July 7 2017 | - | Would have been Aaron's 31st birthday |
| July 8 2017 | - | Birthday celebration for Aaron with his friends and family |

We had a great celebration with balloons, and everyone wrote a note for Aaron, and the family also wrote one for my mom and Emily. We placed the notes in the balloons and filled them with helium and let them go. It was very spiritual and uplifting watching the balloons go up to the sky.

July 11 2017 - Was such a difficult day for me. Jim went to town and I started to clean the house from Saturday's celebration and I just got so depressed and started to cry. It lasted for at least an hour. I looked at Aaron's picture and tried to talk to him. The rest of the day I was on the verge of crying. Around 7:00 p.m., I went to the rooftop patio and wrote a note to Aaron, Emily, and my mom, and placed them each in a balloon and filled them with helium and sent them off into the sky. Aaron's balloon was purple, Emily's orange, and Mom's red. I watched them fly until I could no longer see them. Just doing the balloon release somewhat helped me feel more at ease.

July 14 2017 - We took the motorhome on a trip to Leavenworth, USA, just to get out of the depressing house for a week. Trip was no help. Aaron was with us all the time, which I loved, but I needed a break from the depression. On the last day, July 21, in Penticton, at our campground, which we went to for years with the kids when they were younger, we wanted to place some of Aaron and Emily's ashes at the windmill. Too many people around, so we opted out until September. We did our usual bike ride down the KVR trail and stopped at the pond where we normally do. Jim and I had a good cry, with all the memories coming back to us from when we brought the kids here for seven years and spent all our summers here. We saw a group of young kids playing basketball and playing their boom box. Right away a blonde boy reminded us of Aaron. Then we saw a young boy riding his skateboard; again, it was like looking at Aaron when he was little.

July 31 2017   -   Daniel and I saw a spiritual medium. The spiritual medium left Daniel and me a little satisfied but more confused as to whether it was real or not. She did say some things that she wouldn't have known about Aaron. She told me and Daniel to look for the number 86. This was Aaron's birth year. Also for feathers and dimes and nickels and butterflies. Also, for Daniel to watch for large birds. These would all be signs from Aaron. She said that Jim should watch for electrical noises and that Aaron would be hiding things on him for fun, like tools and keys. Also for him to watch for coins.

She also said that Aaron's grandfather was the one that pulled Aaron up, and that Aaron was the one that pulled Emily up. She said that Aaron was in a beautiful, bright light and that his job in Heaven was to heal other people. He said that he had loved his life here on earth and that he wanted to heal me from being so sad.

When we got home, and I explained to Jim what she had said. I heard a noise come from the dining room, so I proceeded to head to the dining room to see what it was. There was a sympathy card that had fallen, yet the window was not open, so there was no breeze. I still had all the cards standing on the dining room table and the side table. I picked up the card and decided to look at the back of it (don't know why), when I noticed the number 86, along with other numbers on the back of that card. I quickly brought it to the kitchen to show Jim and Daniel. I said, "Aaron is here. He is telling us to believe what the medium told us today."

Well, we all received several coins, and a few of them had the year 1986 on them. Crows were always hanging around the yard and getting pretty close to us. Daniel saw large eagles and other birds. I kept seeing so many beautiful, light-blue butterflies (Aaron's favorite color was baby blue). Feathers— they were always in our path.

One day, Daniel ripped out part of the carpet in the driver's side of his truck so he could install speaker wire. In front of his eyes was a shiny dime with the year 1986.

August 4 2017   -   Heard from our friends that another young man in our town died at the age of 34 to fentanyl poisoning.

August 27 2017   -   Joined a closed group called Moms Stop the Harm, momsstoptheharm.com, a group where family members can talk freely about their loved ones that have passed from addiction or substance abuse, or loved ones that are still alive but battling with addiction. Much help is given from this site because we are all struggling with the same loss. The only problem I have now being a member for four months is every time I turn on my computer, I get another notification of somebody's loved one that has passed from addiction or substance abuse. It starts to get to you after a while. The group has done many good things, and tries to inform and support one another and share information that is too personal for the public Facebook page.

September 4 2017   -   I had a horrible day; drove to town for groceries, couldn't stop crying. (This seems to happen to me a lot, when driving by myself, whether I have music on or not.

Aaron's face always pops into my mind.) The first several months after he passed, I kept getting the vision of him laying in his bed when I first found him. Even when I went to bed at night. I would try to replace that vision with a different one—a happy one—but it didn't work. I wore my sunglasses in the store to block my eyes, swollen from crying. On the way home, the tears started up again. I told Jim when I got home what happened. He told both Daniel and myself from now on, when any of us have a troublesome day because of Aaron, don't hide it. Let's talk about it in the open.

So I drank a bottle of wine to stop the hurt, then went onto Facebook and started to read the good thoughts and wishes Aaron's friends were posting about him, including pictures I had not seen before. There were some good stories that helped cheer me up.

September 5 2017 -   Saw more pictures of Aaron on Facebook, but this time I was startled because a couple of them were selfies that I hadn't seen before. I had a second of a glimmer of hope that he had posted them. But it was quickly washed away by the truth.

September 18 2017 -   Shauna's dog Roxie passed away.

October 3 2017   -   I hate everything today, mad at everything. I hate this world. I want out of my body now! I can't stop crying, no happiness anymore. Nothing matters anymore. I went through a small photo album I made up a long time ago with Aaron's pictures. One picture was with Aaron, Emily, Daniel, and Bev, their grandmother. I couldn't stop crying because Daniel is the only one left in that picture. Everything is going wrong. Princessa came up to me when she saw me crying. I picked her up and she kissed me. I know it won't be long and she will have to be put down because of her congestive heart failure. Life is so senseless!

October 7 2017   -   Elmo, my mom's dog, passed away.
October 8 2017   -   Thanksgiving celebration, no intention of celebrating, nothing to be thankful for. I did make a turkey dinner for Daniel's sake, because Jim and I couldn't care

less. I can't keep pulling them down into my hole. I did tell both Jim and Daniel at dinner that I was grateful for them, but that was it.

October 12 2017   -   Another really bad day. Yesterday a car sideswiped mine. I was so upset, but it really didn't come out until the next day. I went to town for an estimate on my car and on the way home I broke down in tears again. Asking Aaron to please find a way to bring me to him.

October 27 2017   -   Princessa, our dog, passed away of heart failure. (Also within the year my precious dog Shadow passed away Oct 23, 2016, four days before his 16th birthday.)

November 13 2017 -   I went into my exercise gym, which was shared with Aaron's bedroom. First time since he passed. I lasted about six minutes on the elliptical before I broke down and cried uncontrollably. I have family pictures all over the walls and I kept staring at his baby pictures and when he was a young boy.

November 19 2017 - It was seven months since Aaron had passed and it was a really hard day for me. I cried a lot. That day I took my dog (Shih Tzu) into the vet and after the vet I took him to the dog store to buy him a chewy treat. He likes to lay on the floor behind the driver's seat, so I gave him the treat. I didn't expect him to eat the whole thing because it was about a foot long and it was a hard bone. When we arrived home I got him out and looked under the seat for the bone but couldn't find it. So I got a flashlight and looked again. The bone was gone, but I found a dime with the year 1986 on it. I had picked the car up a few days before from the repair shop and they had cleaned it inside and out.

Our son Aaron is still with us. We may not know it all the time. But from time to time he will let us know that he is still here. We miss him like crazy, and I still cry almost every day. I still have three shrines set up for him in the house, and change the flowers constantly and light the candles every night. Not just for Aaron, but for my mom and Emily too.

I don't know what life is going to be like without Aaron; I don' t even want to imagine how it's going to play out. All I know is that we will miss him every day for the rest of our lives. Will the tears ever stop? I doubt it. But eventually it won't be an everyday thing, I'm told. I do know our hearts will always have a large hole that will never heal until we are with him again as a whole family.

The devastation of Aaron's death—and on Daniel's birthday— will haunt Daniel forever. Although he did make a decision to live for both Aaron and himself. On every birthday, Daniel will be doing something adventurist—something that Aaron would have wanted to do—for the both of them, and Aaron will be with him in spirit. I wrote another poem for Aaron today.

Watched his memorial DVD for the first time since his funeral. Couldn't stop crying. I knew I shouldn't have watched it. The only upside today was that I found that dime with the year 1986 under my car seat.

7 MONTHS

Our family chain is broken
There's not much left to say

The void you left is deep
and it was 7 months today

We try so hard to live again
1 step forward, and 2 back with pain

Your friends still post your pictures
I'm so thankful for those days

We continue to cry in our sleep
for missing you is now our life . . . incomplete

The deaths keep happening around us
Our strength is running low

I pray to God that one day soon
Our chain will link again.

Our love for you will never fade
our blood, our son,
you're the gift our precious
love had made.

WE LOVE YOU AARON JAMES

I tried so hard to write into a diary every day but I just couldn't do it. Some days my strength was amazing, and others . . . well, I just didn't have much. So many people have told me that I am strong. I don't think I am as strong as others believe. I just know that I have others here in this physical world that still depend on me, and the last thing I want to do is hurt them with the same hurt we feel for Aaron.

Christmas was exceptionally hard this year. We did not celebrate Christmas the traditional way. We all wanted it that way. There were tears and there were a few laughs talking about memories of Aaron. We are just so glad that the first Christmas without him is over.

Shauna's Medium Reading

December 6, 2017

I went to a group medium reading tonight. There were around 50 people there. She managed to read most people and was very specific with details and she seemed to be very accurate.

I was extremely excited that Aaron came through! She said he wasn't great at communicating but is getting better.

She immediately asked me how Aaron and I connect with the month of July (both our birthdays). She then said that he thanked us for releasing balloons for him.

She said we didn't have children together but we shared a dog who was just like our baby. She even told me he was a bulldog. (I am not joking!!) She said Aaron treated that dog like his own baby and that he thanked me for taking such good care of him since he passed. He said that he knows I've worried that he suffered when he died and he wanted me to know that he didn't suffer and that he was sorry because he didn't want to die and he wanted to say goodbye. She even mentioned that he had tried to text me to tell me how much he loved me before he died (Aaron had an unsent text on his phone that he wrote to me that said "I love you sooo much babes").

She said that he was showing her cupcakes and that it had something to do with our dog (I made cupcakes for Axl's birthday in August). She said that Aaron's dad wasn't well, or that something was wrong with him, and that Aaron has been with him a lot.

Aaron kept telling her that I was beautiful inside and out. He said that I am a strong person who knows what I want and he is going to pick the right person for me to be with someday. She said that he knows that we were each other's "one" and that he's sorry that he died.

Aaron told her that we were wanting to go to Mexico and that he's sorry that he can't be with me when I go. She knew that he had passed away recently. She said that Aaron was going to open doors for me to do something different (either change jobs or start helping people like Aaron). She said that Aaron was telling her that the clunking noise in his vehicle was gone. Aaron leaves a lot of money around the place but I don't really see it, so I will start finding $5.00 bills in random places.

The last thing she said is that Aaron told her I really liked his hair and that it's still the same (the last weekend I spent before Aaron died, he got his hair cut . . . I kept telling him all weekend how much I loved his hair because I didn't like the shaggy look he had for the few months before, so I was encouraging him to keep his hair all nice and groomed like he used to).

She ended the reading by saying that Aaron wants me to know that he really, really loves me.

I think her reading was about 10 minutes, but everything she said was exact. I was completely blown away!!

(Note from Sylvia: Shauna did come to Mexico to visit Jim and me for a week in February of 2018. It was strange at first because we were expecting Aaron to be with her. Shauna also said that a few nights before her flight, she dreamt of Aaron and her on the beach and he was behind her with his arms around her, and she could smell his scent.)

British Columbia CORONER'S REPORT

Ministry of Public Safety and Solicitor General
BC Coroners Service

Case No.: 2017-5034-0002

CORONER'S REPORT
INTO THE DEATH OF

MENNEAR	AARON JAMES
SURNAME	GIVEN NAMES

OF

CHERRYVILLE
MUNICIPALITY OF RESIDENCE

I, Rodney Bricker, a Coroner in the Province of British Columbia, have investigated the death of the above named, which was reported to Coroner Arenlea Felker on the 19th day of April, 2017, and as a result of such investigation have determined the following facts and circumstances:

Gender: ☒ MALE ☐ FEMALE

Age: 30 YEARS

Death Premise: PRIVATE RESIDENCE

Place/Municipality of Death: CHERRYVILLE   Date of Death: APRIL 19, 2017

Municipality of Illness/Injury: CHERRYVILLE   Time of Death: EARLY AM HOURS

MEDICAL CAUSE OF DEATH

(1) Immediate Cause of Death: a) Fentanyl Toxicity

                                  DUE TO OR AS A CONSEQUENCE OF
Antecedent Cause if any: b)

                                  DUE TO OR AS A CONSEQUENCE OF
Giving rise to the immediate cause (a)   c)
above, stating underlying cause last.

(2) Other Significant Conditions
Contributing to Death:

BY WHAT MEANS   Unintentional illicit drug overdose

CLASSIFICATION OF DEATH   ☒ ACCIDENTAL   ☐ HOMICIDE   ☐ NATURAL   ☐ SUICIDE   ☐ UNDETERMINED

Date Signed: JANUARY 8, 2018

Rodney Bricker, Coroner
Province of British Columbia

This document has been prepared pursuant to the authority of the Chief Coroner, Coroners Act, S.B.C 2007 c.15
Section 53(2)
Page 1 of 2

PTC
BC's Provincial Toxicology Centre

Provincial Health
Services Authority
Province-wide solutions.
Better health.

655 West 12ᵗʰ Avenue, Vancouver B.C., V5Z 4R4   Telephone: (604) 707 2715 Facsimile: (604) 707 2717

B.C. CORONERS SERVICE

Coroner FELKER, ARENLEA
103 1420 ST PAUL ST
KELOWNA, BC V1Y 2E6

TOXICOLOGY REPORT

Dr. NICHOLSON, PETER
VERNON JUBILEE HOSPITAL

RECEIVED

NOV 1 6 2017

B.C. CORONERS SERVICE
INTERIOR REGION

Name of Deceased: **MENNEAR, AARON JAMES**

PTC No: **2017-0860**

Coroner Case No: **2017-05034-0002**

Autopsy No: **FV17-41**

The Provincial Toxicology Centre received on 21 April 2017 the following specimens:
: 1 BLOOD (GREY TOP TUBE): 1 BLOOD (RED TOP TUBE): 1 URINE (TUB, UNSTABILISED): 1
VITREOUS (GREY TOP TUBE): 1 VITREOUS (RED TOP TUBE): 1

The results are as follows: (* indicates new result)

BLOOD (GREY TOP TUBE)	R SUBCLAVIAN	*** FORENSIC STAT ANALYSIS ***		
BLOOD (GREY TOP TUBE)	R SUBCLAVIAN	ETHYL ALCOHOL		Not Detected
BLOOD (GREY TOP TUBE)	R SUBCLAVIAN	GENERAL DRUG SCREEN		No other Drugs Detected
BLOOD (GREY TOP TUBE)	R SUBCLAVIAN	FENTANYL	53 nmol/L	0.018 mg/L
BLOOD (GREY TOP TUBE)	R SUBCLAVIAN	NORFENTANYL	6.60 nmol/L	0.002 mg/L
BLOOD (GREY TOP TUBE)	R SUBCLAVIAN	MIRTAZAPINE		Detected
VITREOUS (GREY TOP TUBE)		ETHYL ALCOHOL		Not Detected

Fentanyl level is within a range where therapeutic and lethal
concentrations overlap.

Screening estimates indicate:

~ Mirtazepine level is within a range considered therapeutic.

Aaron Shapiro, Ph.D., Associate Scientific Director

Report issued on 10-November-2017

Exhibits will be discarded after 08-February-2018

BRITISH
COLUMBIA

CORONER'S REPORT
INTO THE DEATH OF

MENNEAR	AARON JAMES
SURNAME	GIVEN NAMES

INVESTIGATIVE FINDINGS

On the evening of April 18, 2017, Mr. Aaron James MENNEAR retired to his bedroom. At 1000 hours, April 19, 2017, a family member found Mr. Mennear in his bedroom unresponsive. BC Ambulance Services attended but no resuscitative efforts were made as death was obvious.

Scene examination revealed drug paraphernalia including used pipes, straws, tin foil and a paper flap containing a brown powder. Prescription medications including pain killers, sleeping pills, and anti-anxiety medications were also revealed.

Investigation into the medical history of Mr. Mennear indicated a snowboarding accident that fractured his left leg. As a result Mr. Mennear had multiple surgeries in 2014 and 2015 and was regularly prescribed opioids. It was reported that when these opioids were cut off, Mr. Mennear began "doctor shopping" to obtain medications. In January of 2017, Mr. Mennear advised his family that he was using heroin and fentanyl.

Mr. Mennear's physician reported that Mr. Mennear suffered from chronic anxiety and heart palpitations. Because of his chronic use of illicit drugs, the physician offered Mr. Mennear the Methadone treatment program, but the offer was refused. Mr. Mennear's last prescription was for mirtazapine, prescribed on February 17, 2017.

POST MORTEM/TOXICOLOGY EXAMINATION

An autopsy was not required as examination of post mortem specimens taken from Mr. Mennear determined a cause of death. Blood samples indicated Fentanyl levels were within a range where therapeutic and lethal concentrations overlap.

CONCLUSION

I find that Aaron James Mennear died in Cherryville on April 19, 2017, due to Fentanyl Toxicity. I classify this death as accidental and make no recommendations.

. . . .
Rodney Bricker, Coroner
Province of British Columbia

SUMMARY

(CBC News, January 31, 2018) More than 1,420 people died of illicit drug overdoses in British Columbia in 2017, the most tragic year ever. (*British columbia Coroners Service Rafferty Baker/cbc*)

Approximately 81 percent of suspected deaths last year involved the opioid fentanyl. Lapointe said it was often combined with other illicit drugs—most often heroin, cocaine, or methamphetamines. (*Lisa Lapointe: Chief Corner British Columbia*)

Nearly 90 percent of people who died were alone inside a home when they suffered an overdose. Four out of five were men, and more than half of all victims were between the ages of 30 and 49.

Vancouver saw the highest number of deadly overdoses last year, followed by Surrey and Victoria.

The coroner's service said nobody died at any supervised consumption site or at any of the drug overdose prevention sites.

The number of deaths in 2017 had surpassed the 2016 record of 993 by October.

March 6 2018

There were 125 people who died of a suspected drug overdose in British Columbia in January. The latest figures from the British Columbia Coroners Service indicate the opioid overdose crisis is showing no sign of letting up, with an average of four per day. The number of deaths went up 25 percent from the previous month, when 100 people died in British Columbia.

However, when comparing January of 2017 to January of this year (2018), the number of overdose deaths actually declined by 12 percent.

Even so, illicit drug overdoses have surpassed other causes of unnatural deaths in British Columbia in 2017 by a significant margin.

More people died of an overdose than in homicides, motor vehicle incidents, and suicides, combined.

The one-year anniversary of Aaron's death is fast approaching; April 19, 2018. I shudder to think how much time has passed already. I don't feel any different; I still miss our son as much now as on the last day we saw him.

We lost so much in 2017. Our son, niece, my mother, and four family dogs. I still can't comprehend any of it. Maybe I'm not supposed to; maybe I'm just supposed to say that's life, and keep living to your fullest until you are called upon. Although I can't. I still try to make sense of all of this; I doubt I will ever get the answer. I am struggling every day with all of this still, and my family is struggling with all of this. I know my husband and sons keep a lot of their feelings hidden inside. I would rather talk about him and have his pictures everywhere. I want people to know that he existed and how special he is. I guess it's just one step at a time, one day at a time. Everyone heals differently. Everyone heals at their own pace. Maybe I will never heal. I know one thing for sure, ever since I was told to write about Aaron, I felt that it is my purpose in all of this tragedy. (If it's the last thing I do, I know in my heart Aaron would approve of this book.)

My goal is to let other families know what they can expect if their child is doing drugs, and how they can know what to look for behaviourally. I know we all want to think our child is perfect and that they would never, ever, wander down that road. No child is perfect; we all need help growing up. So please don't close your eyes to the troubles your child may have.

If I could give one piece of advice, it would be this: if you have children, or know of someone that has, and they have not been themselves behaviourally or in any manner for a time (go back and check symptoms of the drugs), please, please, don't wait and think that they are going through a phase. Check their rooms, their belongings, and keep tabs on them. One year we found a joint hidden inside a pen. The insides of the pen were removed except the ball point. This could be your child. Don't ever say it won't happen to mine. That's what we said!

God Bless You and Yours

I fear for one year is coming near
I fear my memories won't be so clear

You were our little treasure, our little baby boy
You gave us so much pleasure, our little bundle of joy.

You always had a smile and was happy as could be
You were almost the perfect child, but perfect a child
can never be.

You grew up to be a handsome caring young man
You had a heart of gold and from everyone we were told.

For now the angels have my son - they get your smiles and
laughs and hugs that could squeeze a ton.

But in our hearts you will always live
I just wish I could have had one more hug and kiss to give.

Until the day that we all pass - together again we will be
at last.

Forever 30
Loving you Forever and into eternity

Mom and Dad

In 2017, there were 1,422 overdose deaths in British Columbia. That's 43 percent higher than in 2016, which had 914 deaths.

Nearly 30,000 naloxone kits were handed out in 2017 in British Columbia.

British Columbia marks 2017 as the deadliest overdose death year in provincial history.

January 2018 - 125 deaths.

In Loving Memory of our precious son

Aaron James Mennear

July 7, 1986 - April 19, 2017

I am sending a dove to heaven
with a parcel on its wings
be careful when you open it
Its full of beautiful things
Inside are a million kisses
wrapped up in a million hugs
To say how much I miss you
and to send you all my love.

I hold you close within my heart
and there you will remain
To walk with me
throughout my life
until we meet again.

Not a day goes by that we
don't mourn your loss.
We miss you
and love you so much.
Mom, Dad, Daniel,
Shauna and Justin

REFERENCES

My history - Aaron's own words found on his memory stick

Coroners Service British Columbia - Summaries and Graphs

globalnews.ca

cbcNews.ca

theglobeandmail.com

cnn.com

drugabuse.gov/publications/drugfacts/anabolic-steroids

drugabuse.gov/publications/drugfacts/cocaine

drugabuse.gov/publications/drugfacts/heroin

drugabuse.gov/publications/drugfacts/fentanyl

About the Author

I am a mother of three boys, all adults now, and each of them are beautiful and special in their own individual way. My husband, Jim, and I, always did the best we could for the boys. Got them involved in sports, outdoor activities, etc., so they never got bored . We took them camping , and out of the country
on holidays to give them insight on how others in the world lived. Like most parents, we thought everything was fine. Even though we told them that they could always come to us for anything, Aaron still chose not to, out of sheer embarrassment , and look where it led him.

I don't know how our lives will go forward from here. I would not wish this on my worst enemy; it is a life-changer. Since this happened, I have read over 15 books on life after death, and because of what I have learned, I do feel a little better knowing that Aaron is always with us, and that we will be with him again one day. We do receive gifts from Heaven from him, although not as many now as we did in the first few months. But enough to know that he is still watching over us.

His dog, Axl, is now with Shauna, Aaron's girlfriend. I call Axl my grandson because he is the only baby Aaron will ever have.

———————

Daniel, Sylvia (mom), Aaron

Aaron, Jim (dad), Daniel,

Shadow in buggy, Princessa behind plant, Ozzie

Justin, Aaron, Daniel - Brothers

Aaron, Shauna

R,I.P. Our Beloved Son

Love Mom and Dad Forever

Made in the USA
Columbia, SC
08 August 2018